RELUCTANTLY SINGLE

HAROLD IVAN SMITH

RELUCTANTLY SINGLE

*You Can Stop Waiting for Life to Happen
and Start to Live*

ABINGDON PRESS
NASHVILLE

RELUCTANTLY SINGLE

Copyright © 1994 by Abingdon Press

This book is printed on acid-free, recycled paper.

Library of Congress Cataloging-in-Publication Data

Smith, Harold Ivan, 1947–
  Reluctantly single / Harold Ivan Smith.
    p. cm.
  ISBN 0-687-36048-X (acid-free paper)
  1. Single people—United States. 2. Single people—United States—Religious life. I. Title.
HQ800.4.U6S638 1994
305.90652—dc20   94-11826

The excerpt on page 50 is reprinted, with permission, from *A Spirituality of Wholeness: The New Look at Grace,* Copyright © 1988 by William Huebsch, published by Twenty-Third Publications, P.O. Box 180, Mystic CT 06355. Toll free: 1-800-321-0411.

Scripture quotations, unless otherwise noted, are from the New Revised Standard Version of the Bible, copyright © 1989 by the Division of Christian Education of the National Council of the Churches of Christ in the USA. Used by permission.

Those noted NIV are from the *Holy Bible, New International Version.* Copyright © 1973, 1978, 1984 International Bible Society. Used by permission of Zondervan Publishing House. All rights reserved.

94 95 96 97 98 99 00 01 02 03—10 9 8 7 6 5 4 3 2 1

MANUFACTURED IN THE UNITED STATES OF AMERICA

Writing on the question of significance and how one will be remembered is inevitably shaped by the deaths of friends, especially friends who died far too young:

Anne C. Hargrove
Cecil Paul
Leon Doane
Martin King
Billy "Rusty" Esposito

Eternal life has taken on a whole new meaning through their deaths. I dedicate this book to their memory.

92748

ACKNOWLEDGMENTS

Writers seldom do their work in isolation. Ideas must be tested and shaped through spirited dialogue with friends. *Reluctantly Single* has been influenced by such exchanges with Mimi Williams, Linda Quanstrom, Alice Cowan, Kay Collier-Slone, Carole Streeter, Mark Thrash, Elva McAllaster, and Anne C. Hargrove. I owe a special word to Carole Streeter for her editorial input on the early draft of this book.

Writing is also affected by the strength of one's faith community. I owe such a debt to the people of Saint Andrew's Episcopal Church, Kansas City, who take prayer so seriously and who so faithfully prayed for me during this project. And to those wonderful friends who make up the Monday night group who also prayed and encouraged me, I am thankful. This writer has also been affected by the spirited preaching of our rector, Jeffrey Black.

Finally, I owe a real debt to three professors in my doctoral program at Asbury who gave me such latitude to research the issue of significance: Steve Harper, Reg Johnson, and Chuck Killian.

To all, I express my gratitude.

CONTENTS

1 / Single and Reluctant

11

2 / Single and Floating, Fighting, and Navigating

30

3 / Single and Shattered

42

4 / Single and Belonging

51

5 / Single and Relevant

72

6 / Single and Remembered

99

Epilogue: A King and a Pauper

119

Notes

123

1

SINGLE AND RELUCTANT

Perhaps you've heard about the egotist/optimist who was being tarred and feathered and driven out of town. He quipped, "As much as I've always wanted to lead a parade, if it wasn't for the honor of the thing, I'd just as soon pass." That's the way a lot of America's sixty-eight million unmarried people feel about their singleness. "I'd just as soon pass."

Maybe you've read previous books I have written on the subject of singleness: *Positively Single* (Victor), *Single and Feeling Good!* (Abingdon) or *Sleeping Single in a Double Bed* (Harvest House). One fringe benefit of writing these has been to stand at a book table and listen to browsers react to my titles—in many cases, unaware that I was the author. My focus for these years of singleness has been to make the best of it; in fact, to make the *most* of the single season.

WHAT'S WORSE THAN SINGLENESS?

I have long insisted that there are a lot of things worse than being single; for example, being married to the wrong person. Or having your personhood abused on a systematic basis. A friend of mine has concluded, "The only thing worse than not having what you want is having something that you do not want!"

Oscar Wilde observed, "Men marry because they are tired; women because they are curious." I sometimes ask people who come to me for counseling "What ever possessed you to marry this person in the first place?" Listen to the answers:

- I was tired of being single.
- I thought I could change him.
- We'd gone together so long . . .
- He said to me, "I'm not getting any younger and you're not either. Let's give it a whirl. What have we got to lose?"
- I thought I was in love.

Those are the verbalized responses, but other reasons lie in the quiet corridors of hearts that appear to be pretty mangled, hearts that look as though they've been through one of those slicer/dicers they used to sell at the Kentucky State Fair.

A lot of people ask, "How can anyone get used to singleness in a couples' world?" Some people attending my seminars were in a desperate race to beat their ex to the altar. That can be a great way to "pay back" the spouse: "See, somebody loves me!" Over the years, I've listened to tearful tales of loneliness, fear, deprivation, rejection, even ridicule.

I've met my fair share of unlikely single adults—those who are single for a reason. One man called me a "dirty ol' secular-humanist" and as an afterthought added, "probably a Communist" because I spoke so positively of singleness. Someone else politely suggested that I was antifamily. I've had Bible thumpers wave their King James Bible at me wanting to "dialogue" about the issues of singleness. A denominational executive ordered me to tell single adults to "cut out all that sex!"

12

One single adult who didn't like my philosophy on singleness insisted that single programs for single adults should concentrate on inviting "married folk to come and tell about the joys of marriage." That would make about as much sense as bakers showing up at Weight Watchers or Overeaters Anonymous to describe their latest chocolate fudge cake recipe.

No, I don't always find singleness joyful or easy or fun. Most of the time I do; but some days I just have to take singleness an hour at a time.

Recently, I decided not to spend Christmas in Kentucky with my extended family. December 24-25 was shaping up to be a solo holiday. I was second-guessing my decision until a friend called. That call changed my mood when I gave about five seconds thought to the many married adults who were having Norman Rockwellesque Christmas gatherings but had cold, resentful hearts toward their spouses. I thought about some reluctantly single adults who were in second-rate dating relationships at Christmas after concluding that a bad relationship was better than no relationship.

After a glorious Christmas Eve service, I came home, sat by my tree, and opened presents. But Christmas Day was the winner. I called one hotel to make a reservation for brunch only to be gruffly told: "We don't seat parties of one on Christmas Day!"

I called another hotel. "What is the smallest party you can accommodate for Christmas brunch?" "One" the hostess answered. I made my reservation.

Of course, on the drive to the restaurant, I was concerned about a practice most singles detest. Over the loudspeaker, in a crowded waiting area, a single adult's name is called: "Party of One!!!" A single adult gets those "looks" mixing loathing, compassion, admiration, or pity. "Poor dear––too bad he's alone on Christmas. So sad." Besides, many have been to see the annual rendering of the life of December's star single adult: Ebenezer Scrooge. But even Scrooge ends up with a family!

But on that Christmas day I heard only "Smith party" and was shown to a wonderful table by the grand piano. Not bad. En route, I noticed I was not the only "party of one." Hmmm. About halfway through my meal, I happened to observe a family of six enjoying the scrumptious buffet but not one another's company. In fact, *enjoying* is stretching it. They were aggressively eating. I watched in utter amazement. No one talked. I assumed the composition to be mother and father (mid fifties) and a grown son and daughter and their spouses. Six silent adults rigorously chewing. The mother got choked. The family kept eating. They didn't miss a chew. Other patrons helped her, but not one family member stopped eating.

Reflecting on what I had just witnessed, I realized that eating alone on Christmas Day is not sad; eating with a family of unloving individuals is sad.

WHAT WILL YOU SETTLE FOR?

There's nothing wrong with being single and reluctant. But what will you do when you get tired of being single? One friend jokes: "I know what you're *looking* for, but what will you *settle* for?" That's one question all single adults need to ponder. *What will you settle for?*

All of us come to points where we toy with the idea: *this* is the best I can do and we settle for far less than the best. We settle for discount relationships. Some hear a ticking emotional or biological clock, not unlike looking up at the scoreboard during an intense basketball game and realizing that time for a victory is running out.

What about those words of the wedding ceremony: I do? Two simple words. People who hate being single are sometimes tempted to change the I to *you*, add an apostrophe and two Ls. "I do" becomes "You'll do." It happens every day. It happens in Las Vegas rent-a-chapels. It happens in the most pious sanctuaries in the land. Reluctant single adults panic.

ELEMENTS OF AN ATTITUDE ON SINGLENESS

Singleness is a lot like fruitcake. Fruitcakes have basic elements: butter, sugar, flour, baking powder, and eggs. Ninety-six percent of all fruitcakes have those common elements—the only difference is the quantity of each. However, certain specifics make one fruitcake radically different from another. Candied cherries, pineapple chunks, raisins, figs, dates, orange and lemon peels, citron, and nuts. In some, there are "mystery" elements, even well-kept family secrets.

As with the fruitcake, so with the attitude toward singleness. There are basic elements and there are mysteries. I have identified the following basics: (1) beliefs and assumptions, (2) attachments, (3) fears and insecurities, (4) family-of-origin issues, and (5) early exposure to positive role models of singleness.

Beliefs and Assumptions

By this point in life you have some strong beliefs about marriage: is it *a* norm or *the* norm? What price would you pay, what compromise would you agree to, in order to get married? Your beliefs are based on conclusions, some careful, some quite sloppy, that you have made or been forced to make about marriage.

A Man for Every Woman

Some reluctants believe that there is a man for every woman. Simply, too many single adults ignore the numbers. If we loaded the Ark today—and you had to be married to ride—there would still be approximately seven million women on the dock who would watch it sail into the sunset. That's reality!

A Hot Potato Called Homosexuality

A percentage of the population (10 percent according to Kinsey, 14 percent according to Richardson, 2.85 percent according to Guttmacher, 2.8 percent according to the National Opinion Research Center) is identified as homosexual.[1] (It should be noted that Richardson's 14 percent is of the single adult population; the other percentages are of the adult population in general.) Previously, many persons of homosexual orientation married to hide or deny their homosexual preference; also many married young, before becoming fully aware of their same-sex attraction. Although that occurs less frequently today, it is not uncommon, particularly for conservative religious persons. It must be noted that many gays are aware of strong homosexual attraction and believe marriage will change them; some marry because they want children; some women, desperate for marriage, marry gay men with an agenda to convert them. Indeed, in some of the ex-gay ministries, marriage and a child is the "proof" of the program's effectiveness.

Too Busy to Be Married

"Momma's boys" or the "daddy's girls" won't be available until a dominating parent's demise.

One of America's greatest industrialists, steel magnate Andrew Carnegie, actively blended mommyism and workaholism. Carnegie "mounted the ladder of success so fast that he scorched the rungs." He earned $25,000,000 a year (in the days before income tax), yet had time for only one Mrs. Carnegie—his mother. Carnegie was both devoted to his mother and dominated by her. So much so that he and Louise Whitfield endured a three-year secret engagement and only married after Momma Carnegie died in November of 1886. Andrew was fifty-one years old when he married—about the time his colleagues were becoming grandparents.[2]

The Angry Single Men

Then there are the egotists, the workaholics, the rednecks with Neanderthal concepts about grooming, housework, and marriage. This is getting a little depressing—but reality is not always a pretty picture. No wonder women scream, "Where are the men?!!!" And, of course, we cannot ignore the focus of the talk shows: men who cannot commit.

But, believe it or not, there are men who are asking, "Where are the good women?" Women just like the woman that married dear ol' Dad—women who have jobs, not careers. Women who resemble TV's June Cleaver. Women who will adore being called *Hon, Babe, Sugar, Darlin'* and can not only enthusiastically respond to "Get me another beer," but can also anticipate his Lordship's thirst.

I see a lot of angry men—not just in bars but also in the workplace, churches, and particularly in the last male bastion, health club locker rooms—who are genuinely confused about the role of the sexes, dating, intimacy, and equal relationships, and who are tired of being blamed for the problems of the world. Even seemingly good men get with the guys and soon are exchanging accounts of the latest "You aren't going to believe this . . ." putdowns in the battle of the sexes.

Large numbers of the reluctantly single have been influenced at an impressionable age by stints as ring bearers or flower girls, by fairy tales such as *Cinderella,* and by dressing up as brides on rainy afternoons. In junior-high youth groups, some of us were told in the most pious of tones, "Teens, be true, God has someone picked out for you." That fantasy had a nice ring to it; it is easily memorized. It is downright mainstream American to believe there's a man for every woman—to believe that love conquers all. Romance is the backbone of our television, our movies, our music.

In 1906, President Theodore Roosevelt, alarmed by the growing number of bachelors and spinsters, thundered that it was un-American not to want to marry. "The greatest privilege and greatest duty of man is to be happily married, and no other form of success or service, for either man or woman, can be wisely accepted as a substitute or alternative."[3] Reporters challenged Roosevelt to explain his position in light of his recent praise for single-adult reformer Jane Addams, of Chicago's Hull House, as "an example for all other women to follow."

"Well," Roosevelt sputtered, "It is equally foolish and wicked for a man to slur the unmarried woman when he would not dream of slurring the unmarried man."[4] The president was not alone in voicing such promarriage statements. Sam Jones, the leading Methodist evangelist in America at that time, said that next to salvation, the greatest gift God gave was a good wife. The family unit, he declared, was ordained and anyone who challenged its authority was "up to no good." "Whenever I see an old maid, I think some man hasn't done his duty. Whenever I see a bachelor, I think of an old hog!"[5]

Where have your beliefs come from? Take a moment and reflect on your beliefs and assumptions about marriage. Jot them down. Now, beside each notion write down its origin or the name of the person who nurtured that notion—perhaps a Sunday school teacher, a youth minister, a favorite school teacher, a counselor, a coach, or a parent. Who convinced you of your beliefs and assumptions about marriage?

Anthony Walsh, author of *The Science of Love and Its Effects on Mind and Body*, has offered fresh insight into romance and suggests that each of us carries in his or her mind "a unique subliminal guide to the ideal partner, a 'love map' to borrow John Money's phrase."[6]

Drawn from the people and experiences of childhood, the map is a record of whatever we found enticing and exciting—or disturbing and disgusting. Small feet, curly hair. The way our mothers patted our head or how our fathers told a joke. A fireman's uniform, a doctor's stethoscope. All the information gathered while growing up is imprinted in the brain's circuitry by adolescence. Partners never meet each and every requirement, but a sufficient number of matches can light up the wires and signal, "It's love." Not every partner will be like the last one, since lovers may have different combinations of the characteristics favored by the map.[7]

Attachments

Are you attached to "making it"? Some single adults just don't have time to be romantic; it interferes with their fantasies for their career advancement and financial goals. It's dog-eat-dog! In an article entitled "Men at War," *The Wall Street Journal* observed that men who get ahead these days need seventy-hour-plus weeks and are "compulsive and driven, and they don't have intimate relationships."[8] Oh, they occasionally need a date for a sales banquet or for a work-related dinner party: "The boss is having a few people over . . ." *Now* is the time to pour oneself into a career. Work the longer hours, pay the price now; the dividends will only increase. You can always marry at fifty-one like Carnegie.

Have you ever had Lipton tea? Of course you have, but that is only because of a young Scot's attachment to making a name for himself. Thomas Lipton had one passion: his business. At no time in his first thirty-seven years did anything other than making money occupy his thinking. Only later in life, after he was enormously wealthy, did he take up yachting, but again, that was business related (great place for business entertaining). His biographer, Alec Waugh, summed up Lipton's early life in two telling sentences. The story of his business life "can be told in a single phrase: *ceaseless hard work backed by advertising*," and the story of his personal life, "*He had no private life* outside of his devotion as a son. All his time, all his energy were poured into his work." Moreover, "He had no friends, or rather he had only business friends, and those he saw in business hours. There were no other hours."[9]

Attached to the Job

This is a troubling paradox in our society. Once upon a time, in the corporate world, families were the measure of stability; the single adult was viewed, despite the quality of work performance, with a slight tinge of suspicion. One large American insurance company still has "the fishbowl" experience for upwardly mobile managers who have not married by their early thirties. These ambitious young workaholics are transferred to the home office to be watched closely. The vice-president of that company explained that hospitality is a basic element in the career ladder. How would single adults, particularly males, he asked me, entertain? If you liked making $35,000 a year (and spending all of it), how much more you'll like making $40,000 with the next promotion. So, every month, eager but unmarried adults make the move to the corporate "fishbowl." It's only two years.

Indeed, because of corporate mobility and the growing preference of corporations to relocate a single rather than a married employee (it's cheaper and one doesn't have to worry about the career spouse finding employment or being unhappy in the new setting), one has to wonder how many relationships drift and die because one party moves 1,000 or 2,000 miles away. Long-distance relationships are difficult to maintain. Some single adult workaholics have used romance as a "time-out" but once married, resume the workaholic life-style.

Attached to the World View

Some single adults are attached to their world views. The divorced male, financially strapped, who grumbles, "All women are alike!" The woman burned by a husband, zapped by an attorney, wounded by a couple of sexual opportunists concludes, "All men are alike!" (There is a tendency to punctuate such conclusions with an exclamation point.) Their limited, biased, prejudiced world view keeps them from romance unless it is with someone with an equally fractured world view. What would it take for such single adults to detach themselves from their world view?

Ever read the personals? Many start out well. But with each additional word or phrase, the ad eliminates hundreds of potential responders who conclude, "That leaves me out." One recent perusal led me to underline these phrases:

> . . . seeking generous male
> . . . seeks full-figured woman
> . . . seeks Miss Right, SBF, 23-36, who loves sports activities
> . . . seeking short SWF, 300-400 lbs. for fun
> . . . seeking attractive SWF, 18-40, for mature relationship, full of fantasy
> . . . seeking 6' 0" plus DBCF, plump, who enjoys candlelight chili dinners

21

> . . . seeking fun-loving, honest, good-looking coun-
> try boy, 19-26
> . . . seeking man 39-50, who is romantically inclined,
> well off, serious, as well as outgoing
> . . . seeking man willing to spoil a ladyseeking
> . . . financially secure, stable SM, with similar likes
> . . . seeking fun-loving, intelligent SWM 23-32, beast
> for fairy tale relationship
> . . . seeking Prince Charming, over 21, white, N/S,
> with an athletic body

Well, who said that Prince Charming has to have an athletic body or money? Or that Princess Charming has to be petite or Rubenesque? The best personal ad may have been this one:

> 45-year-old knight in shining armor, slightly rusty and battered. Looking for maiden, 30-50, to rescue, and dragons to slay.

As I read the classifieds, especially males seeking females, I notice the key qualifiers, which might as well be in neon: *trim*, *petite*, and *slender*. These imply that no one else need apply.

Attached to Upward Mobility

How attached are you to the concept of marrying upward? Is it possible that you may have to marry someone who makes less money than you or who has less education. Would you marry "beneath" your economic status? How attached are you to marrying someone who is "beautiful" or "handsome" and not just attractive?

Attached to Religious Compatibility

Are you attached to marrying someone who has identical religious viewpoints? No one else need apply. Suppose you are a charismatic neo-Pentecostal? Would you marry a fundamentalist? What about your views on the thorny issue of the submission of women? If you are now in a church that provides full opportunities for women in ministry would you marry someone who believes that a woman's place in the church is in the kitchen and the nursery and teaching children under age six? Would you marry outside your faith? Would you marry a nonbeliever? Would you marry an atheist? Would you marry a divorced person or a single parent with three children?

Are you attached to the American mainstream—no vegetarian, granola eaters need apply? What if Prince Charming works with his hands?

To what are you attached?

Fears and Insecurities

When was the last time you took a fearless inventory of your fears and insecurities? Okay, I'll be honest. Being single in my thirties was great; being single in my forties is okay. Fast-forward to the cake-and-punch retirement party. Will I be as positive about singleness when I am sixty-five or seventy-five as I am now? Will I as enthusiastically endorse the contents of my earlier book *Single and Feeling Good* when I am a senior adult? Will I move into a retirement center with a few possessions and tons of regrets and "if onlys"?

I admit that I do have reservations about growing old alone. Years ago, I sat at a dinner with a married single-adult minister who believed that a major function of single-adult ministry was getting single adults matched up. Wedding showers were a major component of the social calendar for single adults. I discounted his arguments until he took advantage of the fact that I had been entertaining his three-year-old to press for the jugular.

23

He leaned forward. "Tell me, Harold Ivan, when you are sixty-five, won't you want a string of grandchildren hungering to be with *Granddad* Smith?" His words ricocheted like a bull's-eye-drawn arrow.

I thought a minute.

"You know, don't you," I began in rebuttal, "there is no guarantee that this boy will grow up to fit the American dream? This boy *could* break your heart. This boy could lead to strings of sleepless nights; police cars parked in your driveway at all hours of the night. There is no guarantee your wife will stay with you or will be there to hold your hand when pain is racing through your body. She could die first. Life doesn't have any guarantees."

As a single adult what do you fear? Growing old alone? Being poor? Being homeless, a bag lady? Being an invalid? Dying young? Never marrying?

What are the sources of insecurity in your life? Your body? Your health? Your education? An arrest? A shadow you pray to God nobody ever uncovers? Your weight, your height? Haven't you stood in front of the bathroom mirror after a shower and moaned, "If only my _____ were _____." Fears and insecurities become the menacing monsters that lurk just beyond; some of us have creative imaginations that lead us to catastrophizing!

Family-of-Origin Issues

All it takes is one afternoon of watching the talk shows to know that June and Ward Cleaver were phantoms. Ever thought your family was a mess but felt just a little relieved after watching an episode of "The Oprah Winfrey Show"? "At least my family's not that bad!" you mutter.

Dysfunctional has become the dominant word in our vocabulary when it comes to family. My family can out-dysfunction your family! Yet, others of us twist to a point of ridiculousness the commandment, "Honor your father and mother that your days may be long upon the earth." To admit anything less than "I came from a *wonderful* family" is to be disloyal or ungrateful.

When it comes to family of origin, some of us have selective memories. There's a wonderful description of such a single adult in Armistead Maupin's novel *Maybe the Moon*.

> Jeff has become increasingly prone to creative remembering. I don't mean that he lies; he just arranges the facts more artfully than anyone I've ever known. In fact, as in his work, he's not so much a writer as a rewriter, endlessly shifting the facts to give more form and function. I've learned to take his memories, as well as his projections, with a few zillion grains of salt.[10]

Many single adults do not want a marriage like their parents had—a cosmetically "puffed" relationship. Maybe you grew up in one of those families with major-league secrets: someone was a fondler or an alcoholic or abusive or a tyrant. Yet, no one outside the family ever saw that. Your family carefully applied the makeup to hide the blemishes, anxious that someone would stumble onto the truth.

Maybe you grew up in a family with minor-league secrets, just nasty little bad habits. Some families never have the police in the driveway to settle a domestic disturbance, but have turned silence and manipulation into an art form. You remember slammed doors, ruined meals, and spoiled family gatherings. You may well have been the glue that held your parents' marriage together.

What did your family of origin teach you about love? Marriage? Sexuality? Faith? Honesty? Take a moment and jot down some lessons learned in your family. What have you pretended not to know about your family? How has your family's reality affected your views of singleness?

Early Exposure to Positive Role Models

One of the best-kept secrets in American cultural history is the influence single adults have had.

What would Christmas be like without the great music written by George Frideric Handel: *Messiah* and "Joy to the World"?

We'd still be traveling by train if it had not been for two single-adult brothers, Wilbur and Orville Wright, who flew the first plane at Kitty Hawk.

Would there be an American Navy without a single-adult admiral named John Paul Jones?

Would there be such widespread use of computers without a single adult named Admiral Grace Hooper?

What would Washington, D.C. look like today if a single adult, Pierre L'Enfant, had not laid its design when the district was little more than swampland?

How advanced would America's medical and scientific community be if a single adult, Johns Hopkins, had not founded his great university committed to research?

Where would thousands of Bostonians go on summer nights if a single adult, Peter Fanueil, had not built his great hall on the wharf?

In what nation would Indiana, Illinois, and Michigan be, if a great unmarried general, George Rogers Clark, had not prevailed in the battle for the Northwest Territory?

Would you have voted in the last election if a courageous single adult, Harry T. Burn, had not stood and cast the deciding vote in the Tennessee Legislature in 1920 to ratify the Susan B. Anthony Amendment to the U.S. Constitution, giving women the right to vote in federal elections?

Would we even have the word *muckraker* in our vocabulary if it had not been developed by a single-adult journalist, Ida Tarbell, to describe the corporate excesses and greed of Standard Oil?

Would Texas still be part of Mexico if it had not been for the vision of a single adult, its first governor, Stephen F. Austin?

Shall I go on? Inventions, movements, gadgets, art, reforms, institutions, music—so many creative gifts of single adults, some of whom were as reluctantly single as you. Francis Bacon said in 1625:

> He that hath wife and children hath given hostages for fortune, for they are impediments to great enterprises, either of virtue or mischief. Certainly the best works and of greatest merit for the public have proceeded from the unmarried or childless men, which both in affection and means have married and endowed the public.[11]

Most of us are woefully ignorant of the contributions single adults have made—without the pressure of family or in some cases, as single parents in an age when women could not vote, own property, have credit, or run for office, blessings we take for granted. They have made our singleness so much easier. Hosts of single adults overcame the prejudice to become nurses and to make nursing an honorable profession for women. Hosts of single adults took on the problems of the cities and made social work an honorable profession.

Think back to the first time you heard these labels: widow or widower; divorcée; single parent; unmarried mother; bachelor; unclaimed blessing; or spinster. What was the tone of voice that accompanied the term: positive or negative? Condescending or judgmental? Deep in the corridor of our hearts, those earliest memories shaped our appreciation or our distrust or disgust for single adults. Were the phrases of sympathy soaked with pity: "Such a tragedy!" Were there under-the-breath utterances, mumblings, raised eyebrows? Most of those labels have telltale fingerprints of deeper meaning.

Consider Truman Capote's description of his "old maid" friend Miss Sook Faulk:

> In addition to never having seen a movie, she has never: eaten in a restaurant, traveled more than five miles from home, received or sent a telegram, read anything except the funny papers and the Bible, worn cosmetics, cursed, wished someone harm, told a lie on purpose, let a hungry dog go hungry. Here are a few things she has done, does do: killed with a hoe the biggest rattlesnake ever seen in this country (sixteen rattles), dip snuff (secretly), tame hummingbirds (just try it) till they balance on her finger, tell ghost stories (we both believe in ghosts) so tingling they chill you in July, talk to herself, take walks in the rain, grow the prettiest japonicas in town, know the recipe for every sort of old-time Indian cure, including a magical wart-remover.[12]

Now compare Capote's experience with the account of a single aunt written on Valentine's Day 1993 by Dianne Aprile in *The Louisville Courier-Journal*. She called Valentine's Day "A Singular Holiday." What did she mean? Everyone knows that Valentine's Day is a couples' day. Dianne talks about a Derby Day in the 1950s. An eight-year-old girl went on a walk, to a cemetery of all places, with her aunt, "a single woman just the other side of thirty—an 'old maid,' as she calls herself."

These two were comfortable with each other from numerous duck feedings, browsing in the shops along Bardstown Road and Baxter Avenue, and high-caloric butterscotch sundaes at Walgreen's soda fountain. Aprile noted, "I feel lucky to have grown up in a family where singles— male and female—were an integral part of extended-family life."[13]

The approach of [Valentine's Day] never fails to send me searching for tokens of love to send to my aunt— who for as long as I have known her has never been a part of a couple in the conventional sense.

I'm sure the mantel over my aunt's fireplace is covered with valentines today.

She has never truly been a single person, if that means "unattached." She has been coupled all her life with friends, with siblings, with neighbors, with co-workers, with nieces and nephews.

At 78, she still walks to neighborhood stores—only now it's often hand-in-hand with my son, who's about the age I was when we trekked to Cave Hill.

I have watched them some days in her backyard, ghosts playing all around them. There's my grandmother, shaking out clothes before hanging them on the line. My uncle sits on a stool, cleaning fish by a pond. My mother, in a halter top, trims weeds by the fence.

My aunt took care of all three of them when they were dying.

I asked her once how she felt about this role. She looked at me like I was 8 years old again and said, "It's what you do for the people you love."[14]

Dianne Aprile's understanding of singleness was shaped by a single aunt. We were not supplied details: if there had been a young man who had not returned from war, or a man who had married another and left her heart forever shattered. Perhaps she was reluctantly single; perhaps it was by her own choice.

Is it possible that in some distant day someone will write about you so poignantly?

Only if you come face to face with the realities of being reluctantly single.

2

SINGLE AND FLOATING, FIGHTING, AND NAVIGATING

He was one of the world's richest men. Certainly, this country's richest single adult. He had it all. His own magazine, *Forbes*; Elizabeth Taylor as friend and date; the confidence of presidents, tycoons, and politicians. In fact, his biography was entitled *The Man Who Had Everything*. Despite his wealth, and like many single adults, Forbes had his share of questions about his niche in the world at any given moment and in posterity.

In 1984, as Malcolm Forbes emerged from a tour of the pyramids, he asked an aide, "Do you think I'll be remembered after I die?" Staffers knew the kind of answers he wanted to hear.

The staffer responded, "Well, you'll at least be an entry in the encyclopedia."

"Double your salary!" Forbes quipped and walked away, laughing.[1]

Forbes magazine had made a name for itself ranking the fortunes of America's richest families and companies. Malcolm knew, however, that fortunes rise and fall. One could have economic and social significance, security, and status today and be down-and-out tomorrow.

Some readers know that reality. Five years ago, a year ago, six months ago you were *un*single. Married. The thought of singleness was the last thing on your mind. Other readers have never been married and are just beginning to question this season called singleness. In some of the most amazing moments, questions drop into our consciousness. All of us have stories, explanations, reasons for our singleness. All of us have, in the words of psychologist Dan McAdams, a *remembered* past, a *perceived* present, and an *anticipated* future.[2] Through these three arenas, we ask questions.

Will I have a job Monday morning?
How much longer will my junk car make it?
Where in the world is Prince Charming?
Whatever happened to commitment?
What if I never have kids?
How will my kids turn out after what they've been
    through?
Why am I single?
What did I do to deserve this?
How do I keep body and soul together?

Questions. We all have them. Answers? That's another subject. Very few answers, I'm afraid.

Increasingly, thoughtful single adults are wrestling with more existential questions:

Who am I?
    Why am I here?
        Where did I come from?
            Where am I going?
                Does God exist?
                    If God exists does it make any difference?

31

If God exists why didn't he keep ____ from
 happening?
Will it matter that I existed?[3]

SIGNIFICANCE

Significance is a major topic of concern among adults of
all ages, although they seldom, if ever, verbalize their
thoughts, except maybe at the weddings of younger sis-
ters/brothers, nieces/nephews, or close friends. The issue
cuts across all sociological measures: race, color, creed,
sexual orientation, and religious preference. The question
has become more acutely familiar because of the large
number of boomers who have slammed up against that
immovable reality called mid-life.

Some of us have never made it to the land of "ooohs and
ahhhs" of marriage. A newspaper story captured my attention and underscores the dilemma of many singles. A
woman had walked down the aisle twenty-one times but
only as a bridesmaid. She had spent over $7,000 on brides-
maids' dresses and shoes.

Some of us have been married and now find ourselves
exiled to the land of singleness. This was definitely *not* the
way the fairy tales said it would turn out. Whatever happened to "and they all lived happily ever after"?

HOW WILL I BE REMEMBERED?

The big question facing so many single adults is: How
will I be remembered? Will my children realize how much
I sacrificed as a single parent to give them a good life? If I

am not married and have no children, who will remember me?

In Fenton Johnson's novel *Scissors, Paper, Rock,* Miss Camilla, the old maid who had lived next door to the Hardin family for years, observed to Raphael, a young unmarried: "Your mother and father . . . out of their love came you and all your brothers and sisters. This is the chain of being, that breaks and reforms and continues itself in ways of its own devising. I am a dead end—I have no issue; I have nothing to pass on."[4]

Who cares that you ever lived? Does it matter that you wrote or made civic contributions or gave generously in time or money to charities or parented a child or started a business or served as a volunteer or were a good neighbor and honest citizen? How does one become significant?

Perhaps significance doesn't just happen. I think Phillip L. Berman was right when he observed, "We live in a time when a number of people are hungry for meaning but have not the courage to seek it."[5] We live in a time when a number of people don't have the foggiest idea where to even look for significance. What they do know is that all they have accumulated, all they have worked to acquire, could be lost to a swift-moving thief or a catastrophic disease. All this wealth was supposed to have at least soothed the search for meaning.

But it hasn't. Yet.

SIGNIFICANCE AND FAITH

Some people of the Christian tradition have historically, and somewhat smugly, confronted the issue with the question from the Westminster Catechism, "What is the chief end of man?" For centuries the answer has satisfied, "To glorify God and to enjoy Him for ever."[6]

But the problem today is that God is not "in" in this culture, although "Higher Power" clearly seems to be holding its own. Furthermore, "catechism" sounds rather imposing, inconvenient, and archaic.

How do you "enjoy" God? Especially the God most of us grew up hearing about? The God who was always about half ticked-off with most of human civilization? The God who was there to "get you" either today or at some distant point? The God who has some of the most ungod-like field reps saying and doing some of the most outrageous things!

Most of us who struggle with this issue of significance grew up in an era when prayer was one of our daily routines: collecting milk money, doing homework, pledging allegiance. Many of us learned the Lord's Prayer but these days, many of us prefer the *revised* Lord's Prayer:

My kingdom come!
My will be done!
On earth or wherever *I* happen to be at the moment!

And a generation of single adults who gave up on the church, who find the church to be the last place on earth they can be themselves or be honest about their struggles, now think that the major purpose of Sunday morning is to catch up on sleep or to read the Sunday paper and have a nice brunch. Paradoxically, some of these eventually find themselves sitting in circles (ironically, often in church basements!) talking about addictions and cravings and loneliness and the meaninglessness of their lives, desperately hoping one of these fellow strangers will listen all the way to the end of the sentence, because most of the key people in their lives do not. When everyone has had a chance to say something, they stand, join hands, and mumble something that sounds a lot like the old version of the Lord's Prayer.

Then, they walk out into the night, still lonely, still addicted, and still feeling insignificant.

Sadly, many discount or counterfeit versions of meaning compete with the real thing for the minds, hearts, and wills of single adults.

SIGNIFICANCE IN AMERICAN CULTURE

Many people in our culture, even today, think meaning is found in pursuing and achieving "the American dream": home in the 'burbs, picket fence, 2.3 kids (healthy, intelligent, well-mannered and drug-free), an IRA, a boat in the driveway, the right club memberships, the right vacation, enough getaway weekends, bragging rights about "what a killing I made on that one!" However long the strand or how glittering the trinkets, one unexpressed wish exists for the elusive quality called significance.

Not a few of us who took it for granted that we had significance—at least with the people we worked with or the child we parented—wonder if someday someone might reveal our inadequacies, our failures, our insensitivities.

Just about the time you think your marriage is significant, you can find yourself sitting in a divorce recovery group in the basement of a church, shaking so badly you pray you won't spill your coffee or your guts and make a scene.

Just about the time you think your parenting skills are significant, your kid can break your heart.

Just about the time you think you have significance in the workplace, your company can be bought, sold, downsized, or junked in a matter of days. Your new boss could be some kid just out of graduate school with a freshly printed MBA and goals for productivity (and significance) that you will never be able to satisfy.

If you think your résumé has significance, drop it in the stack with all the others competing for a job, and remember that at your age you will cost them too much money.

SIGNIFICANCE AND YOUR DECISION

How you will be remembered is a direct result of how you choose to live. It's likely the result of a thousand little decisions. Some think significance will be defined or achieved in some great and glorious crossroad of life, when from deep within we summon sufficient courage to right some wrong, to stand up for what is right, to come to someone's aid or rescue. So, while we keep waiting for the big moment, the big opportunity, we miss the hundreds of little ones that fill our days. And tragically, too many miss those moments because we are so focused on our singleness and the tardiness of Mr. or Ms. Right.

Many of us as children learned the classic prayer,

> Now I lay me down to sleep,
> I pray the Lord, my soul to keep,
> If I should die before I wake
> I pray the Lord my soul to take.

IF I SHOULD DIE BEFORE . . .

Ironically, that prayer, even among those who would be reluctant to define themselves as religious, still springs into our minds. Today, the last half is modified to read, "If I should die before I *achieve* . . ." "If I should die before I *marry . . .*" "If I should die before I *make it*" or "If I should I die before my *talent/work is recognized . . .*" Once we toy with that thought—even for an instant—it becomes a haunter, stalking us, ready to pounce on us in an unguarded moment. "If I should die before I _____." Do you recognize that thought, that question? You may state it a bit differently, but is that not *the* question?

Evelyn Underhill cuts through to the heart of our fascination with more-bigger-better-best:

> We mostly spend [our] lives conjugating three verbs: to Want, to Have, and to Do. Craving, clutching, and fussing, on the material, political, social, emotional, intellectual—even on the religious—plane, we are kept in perpetual unrest: forgetting that none of these verbs have any ultimate significance, except so far as they are transcended by and included in, the fundamental verb, to Be: and that Being, not wanting, having and doing, is the essence of a spiritual life.[7]

I think Underhill has been eavesdropping on my life or snooping in my appointment book. Those three verbs—want, have, do—keep me on the run, keep me longing for ninety-minute hours and thirty-six-hour days to get more done. Those three verbs exhaust me so that I do not have time to think about the realities of my singleness.

Moreover, in this day of hyperfamilism, some contend that marriage/family is *the* essence of significance. Venetia Flaxton captured the mood of many single adults when she complained in the novel *Scandalous Risks*:

> Don't tell me I'm so lucky, so rich, so privileged. Don't talk to me about the starving millions in India, I don't want to know about the starving millions in India, I need all my strength to survive my own starvation, because what's the point of being rich and privileged if you're not loved, and I've never been loved.[8]

SIGNIFICANCE AND NAVIGATORS

I have been impressed by a metaphor developed by Kevin McCarthy in *The On-Purpose Person*. Let's compare singleness to a river. "Some stretches of the river are smooth and quiet; other parts are turbulent and filled with rapids. Most of the river is an endless converging and mixing of currents and conditions that inevitably move you along."[9]

What I conclude from McCarthy is that reluctantly single adults will react in one of three ways.

Floaters: passively resign themselves to accept the river in its present condition. They are obsolete. They aimlessly go along for the ride. And they endlessly complain about how unfair the river is. Floaters like to gripe.

Fighters: fight the forces of nature to take charge of their singleness. They have little control of the river. They experience burnout, stress, depression, and addiction—trying so hard to control the river.

Navigators: recognize we can't control the river; the best we can do is to navigate; prepare and learn to read the river. "We accept the givens and attempt to respond effectively and efficiently to the best of our ability. We do value navigational 'skills'."[10]

As soon as I heard McCarthy's paradigm I realized its implications for single adults. Now instead of asking, Are you never-married, divorced, or widowed? I want to know, "Are you a floater, a fighter, or a navigator?"

Reluctantly Single is directed mainly to the navigators. But if you are still a floater or a fighter, keep reading. Although the navigation of singleness will lead some through blind alleys, detours, occasional panicked feelings of lostness, perhaps despair, the journey can also lead to an intense resolve to be significantly single.

THE PURSUIT OF SIGNIFICANCE

The pursuit of significance can lead us to the decision to live life more fully in the here and now rather than worry so excessively about our past or a delayed future.

The pursuit of significance may lead some of us to the decision to risk our hearts in ways that we have never allowed.

At the end of *Scissors, Paper, Rock,* Miss Camilla, after a lifetime of regrets, speaks out on her life:

> And what is a moment of grace? I lived by guarding my heart—I saw no other choice—but in every long life moments come when our guard is lowered and what we are given is a moment of grace, a chance to forgive.[11]

We are given the chance to forgive those persons, institutions, circumstances, and events that have *caused* us to remain or become single.

Hendrika Vande Kemp and G. Peter Schreck have determined that single adults often understand the question of identity relationally, defining it in terms of something or someone to whom/which they belong.[12] Vande Kemp and Schreck conclude that balanced relationships, with self and others, can only be launched from what they call "the solid place." The solid place is the home of "the solid self" who says convincingly, "This is who I am, what I believe, what I stand for, and what I will do or will not do."[13]

I hope to convince you through our time together in *Reluctantly Single* that you don't have to be married or wealthy or healthy or beautiful or handsome or intelligent or physiologically endowed to have significance. But you do have to be willing to risk your heart.

SIGNIFICANCE AND THE "ENTIRELY OBSCURE"

As long as communities of faith suggest, "If only you were married . . . " many single adults will never achieve their potential. Paradoxically, that faith community will be impoverished by their lack of vision or courage.

Truly significant single adults can often be found in the unnamed, unrecognized multitudes of the unmarried who lived their lives in service to the Single Adult who walked through Palestine and walks the corridors of time inviting all to "come follow me." Often these single adults have no place in our histories, and indeed, few have monuments to their lives, but they richly deserve our thoughtful remembrance.

Gregory Dix observed:

> To those who know a little of Christian history probably the most moving of all the reflections it brings is not the thought of the great moving events and the well-remembered saints, but of those innumerable millions of entirely obscure faithful men and women, every one with his or her individual hopes and fears and joys and sorrows and loves—and sins and temptations and prayers—once every whit as vivid and alive as mine are now. They left no slightest trace in the world, not even a name, but have passed to God utterly forgotten.[14]

Southwest Trafficway and 33rd is a busy Kansas City intersection. I know. I go through it twice a week en route to the airport. Some mornings I didn't see the senior single-adult school crossing guard. Later, he was there, during rush-hour traffic, in the rain, snow, heat, wind, helping children cross. Max defined his job as more than that. This seventy-year-old waved to and smiled at thousands of downtown-bound commuters each school day.

"They say it makes their day. I guess some people get so amazed seeing some goofy guy waving at them," Max once told a reporter.

Max had no wealth, no advanced degrees, no prestige, no power, no key civic memberships. Max was just an older single waving enthusiastically, five days a week, at people desperately chasing significance. Yet, when he died, the *Kansas City Star* editorialized him, something the paper has not always done for the movers and shakers of our city, whom one would assume merited editorial farewell. Max's special kind of service was rare and wonderful.[15]

I miss waving back. So do thousands of my fellow Kansas City residents. They replaced the school guard, but they could not replace Max.

How can I live as a reluctantly single adult in such a way that I will be remembered?

Perhaps Emily Dickinson was not far afield when she penned:

> If I can stop one heart from breaking
> I shall not live in vain;
> If I can ease one life the aching,
> Or cool one pain,
> Or help one fainting robin
> Unto his nest again,
> I shall not live in vain.[16]

41

3

SINGLE AND SHATTERED

S everal times a week I used to drive by a particular old mansion, which I assumed was unoccupied. Dilapidated and run-down, faded newspapers covered many of the windows. But I could tell that in its heyday the house had been elegant.

The house had been built as a wedding present for a young couple whose wedding was to be *the* social event of the year, linking two of the city's finest families. On the wedding day, the church was packed with the city's movers and shakers and social elite. The groom's family was there; the bride's family was there. The groomsmen and bridesmaids were there. The minister and musicians were there. The bride was there. At first, everyone assumed that the groom was just late. The talented musicians kept playing; a few guests squirmed. Eventually, the bride concluded that he wasn't coming. How would she survive such humiliation?

The bride and her sister walked out of the church, stepped into the limousine, and were driven to the mansion. The sisters walked in, locked the door, and never came out again.

Until recently, broken engagements and jilted brides were shameful. Indeed, many fiancées never married after the death of their fiancés; in honor of their memory, these women became reluctantly single. Catherine Beecher, who initiated the use of single women as "school marms" in the American West was such a woman. She could not marry after her fiancé, Hamilton Fish, drowned in a boating accident. Engagements were taken so seriously that, in cases other than death, the abandoned person could sue for breach of contract and collect monetary damages.

Why are you reluctantly single? For some, the answer is a mystery. Others have no good explanation. Others have had an incident—*the* incident. If you knew the details, you would understand. But for some the incident or explanation is unspeakable. They are unable to wrap words around their pain.

My doctoral dissertation studied the role of storytelling in resolving grief following the death of a best friend. The thrust of my research could be summed up as, "You tell me your story and I'll tell you mine." Storytelling also has a place in single-adult ministry.

EXPRESS THE REALITY OF WHAT HAS HAPPENED TO YOU

Tell your story! Remember Archie Bunker's caustic words to Edith: "Stifle yourself!" One of the great blessings of our world today is the growing number of skilled compassionate, caring social workers, psychologists, therapists, pastoral counselors, and lay helpers who will listen all the way to the end of the sentence. Yes, you may have to pay for their ears, but remember this valuable time is an investment in yourself!

Maybe you have had this experience. You start to tell your story, but about one-quarter of the way into it, the listener interrupts, "Oh, I know just what you mean. The same thing happened to me . . . " Suddenly your story is not being told, let alone heard. You have become the listener.

Or have you tried telling your story to a contemporary Pharisee. Part of the way into the story you hear, "You know what your problem is? I'm going to tell you. This happened because you were not living close to God." Or they unleash a string of Scripture verses, some hardly appropriate for your situation. Dietrich Bonhoeffer rightfully concluded, "The first service that one owes to others in the fellowship consists in listening to them."[1] Unfortunately, many single adults have no active listeners in their lives.

Too often we suggest the psychologically equivalent of "Take two aspirin and get some rest . . . you'll feel better in the morning."

REVISE YOUR ASSUMPTIONS ABOUT THE WORLD

Confronted by so many tragedies and injustices, some have demanded, "How could a good God let such a thing happen?" This is supposed to be a "fair" world. Where is it chiseled in granite or bronze: THIS IS A FAIR WORLD?! One of my favorite authors is Rabbi Harold Kushner, who wrote the best seller *When Bad Things Happen to Good People*. The title alone delivers a major dose of reality: bad things *do* happen to "good" single adults! Which also means good things happen to "bad" single adults. The entire book of Psalms could be summarized in a sentence: "Life is hard, but God is good!"

TOLERATE THE EMOTIONAL SUFFERING WHILE NURTURING YOURSELF PHYSICALLY AND EMOTIONALLY

This concept won't sit well with single adults addicted to pain-killers. When we get a headache do we ask, "What is causing this?" Hardly. We reach for a pain-killer, extra strength. Our culture is a denying culture. Pretend that "it" isn't there. Alan Wolfelt tells widows and widowers, Don't make any big decisions, don't sell the house and move to Phoenix two weeks after the funeral. That's sound advice for those who have never married, divorced persons, and single parents too, after a loss or painful time. Give yourself time to heal.[2]

But I don't want to hurt.

I won't say that hurt will do you good, but good can be found in hurt.

We're a replacement society, particularly single adults. Just look at the statistics on divorce. Three out of four men remarry within fourteen months of a divorce—some going from the frying pan into the fire—which could explain why we have high second-divorce rates.

Dr. E. V. Hill, a prominent black clergyman in Los Angeles, has a tremendous following, partly because he is often on cable television. Lots of people watch his spirited preaching and decide to go see him in person. People show up at his church and say, "Brother Hill, you are a man of God. My problem will be solved *if* you pray for me." Dr. Hill, a graciously compassionate minister, is also a realist.

"I say to them—before I pray," Dr. Hill reports, "now there are a couple of things I need to tell you. One, I loved my wife and she was sick. Two, I prayed for my wife and she died! Now, knowing that, do you *still* want me to pray for you?"

A common response is, "Dr. Hill, I feel much better already. I really do. Just coming here and talking to you has made me feel so much better." Dr. Hill calls these folks "quickaholics." They want a "quick fix" to a tough problem.

I have heard recently divorced people say, "How long am I going to feel this way?" My answer—"Oh, a couple of years"—has been known to send them into rage. "Two years! Did you say *two years*?"

45

"Maybe three," I add.

"But he's (she's) already remarried," they counter. "I can't live two years feeling like this!"

I wish I had a magic wand, a formula, a potion, a program to zap away the assorted emotional pains of single adults. But I would not be doing anyone a favor by trying to remove the pain. As they say at my health club, "No pain—no gain!"

CONVERT THE INCIDENT FROM PRESENCE TO MEMORY

Ever get a good scab? Something about a scab draws our attention, like a little canker sore in our mouth. We just can't leave it alone. Probe and wince! Ouch! Probe and wince! With our scabs, we use our fingernails to trim it down, dodging some "light" pain. Parents scold children, "Leave the scab alone!" Too many single adults cannot resist the scabs on their emotions!

What about your emotional scabs, about three feet down on the lining of your soul? The ones that produce so much of the "Baby, you hurt me so baaaad!!!" kind of lyrics.

On my tape player I have three well-used buttons: stop, rewind, play. For my dissertation, I had to transcribe hours of tapes of my subjects talking about best friends who had died. Sometimes because of their emotion, I couldn't clearly understand the words. I would hit the stop button, then rewind, then play. I thought I would wear out the mechanism: Stop-Rewind-Play.

Ever get into that process on sleepless nights: Stop-Rewind-Play? He said . . . , she said . . . , if only I had said. . . Many amateur playwrights write in bed, late at night, "I should have said . . . "

VCR technology has enhanced this process with the introduction of the pause button. Freeze the pain on the screen. I recall this idea illustrated in a wonderful cartoon in Jerry Jamblosky's best seller *Love Means Letting Go of Fear*! Inside a man's head, a theater marquee has these words: NOW PLAYING . . . OLD TAPES!

An incident or circumstance that has hurt you, that has caused you to be reluctantly single and to remain so, has to be converted from presence to memory.

Too many reluctantly singles cannot give up their claim checks for "justice" or the "pound of flesh" they crave. They fantasize by the hour of the shoe being on the other foot. Or of someone paying "big-time" for all the pain they have caused.

I find that many of us try to hide from pain. That's one reason why singles bars are popular. Drown your anger, sorrow, loneliness, hurt, woundedness, fragileness, whatever. Many reason that the loud, dark, smoke-filled bar beats going through the pain alone.

Healing generally needs our cooperation. Some of us become codependent on the hurt. I've met some pretty angry divorced people, angry enough to . . . Increasingly, I am alarmed by the reports of courtroom shootings. People can get trapped in the adversarial judicial system and plot their revenge. "If I can't have you, *nobody* is going to have you!" And there are other characters in the dramas. More and more, single parents use and abuse their children in high stakes power games with an ex-spouse.

There has to come a time when you make the decisions that will facilitate what happened becoming memory rather than presence. In your case, it may not be wedding pictures but the family photo albums and videos that provoke the flow of tears. But it may also be the family pictures that keep you from converting the experience from presence to memory. That was then. This is now.

RECONCILE OURSELVES TO THE EXPERIENCE

When I first started speaking to single-adult groups in the seventies, I was so naive. I actually told people, "Get over it." I had some neat little 1-2-3s for getting over all the hurts and wounds of singleness. I said, "I got over my divorce, so can you." Nice, packaged formulas.

Looking back, I wince. I am glad some of those books are out of print, that some of those cassettes are no longer available. Alan Wolfelt and others have helped me see that you don't get over things, events, experiences, losses, or wounding. You *reconcile* yourself to them.

I am not saying that you have to be glad that you went through divorce or the death of a spouse or whatever circumstances caused you to be reluctantly single. But I am certain that I am a better person for having been down that trail. I learned lessons through that experience that could not have been learned as effectively in other ways. Life got my attention. My friend Linda Quanstrom has phrased it so eloquently:

> There is no wound that Jesus cannot heal
> There is no history that Jesus cannot redeem.[3]

I wish I could tattoo that reality on your eyelids or on the canyon walls of your heart.

There is *no* wound . . . *no* history.

Guess what? Jesus wants you to join a host of reluctantly single adults who can testify to the accuracy of Quanstrom's words. Not that they love being single; but that they have come to terms with their wounds and histories and can now more clearly see their opportunities and possibilities.

What's the difference in these five "needs" and the 1-2-3s that I offered a decade ago? These are tasks or agendas. Realities if you will.

A CASE STUDY FROM GENESIS

I'd like to close this chapter with a brief recall of a Genesis story about Joseph, a Hebrew, who was sold into slavery by his brothers. If anybody had a big-time dysfunctional family story for Oprah, it was Joseph! As a slave in Egypt, Joseph gained the attention of one of Pharaoh's top lieutenants and acquired quite a responsible position in the court, only to lose it in a maliciously false rape charge schemed by his master's wife. So, Joe spent a couple of years in an Egyptian prison for something he did not do.

More years passed. Because of Joseph's reputation as an interpreter of dreams, the Pharaoh summoned him from prison, and Joseph successfully explained the Pharaoh's dream. He became a powerful aide to the Pharaoh, not unlike a Chief of Staff in the White House. A true rags-to-riches miniseries, if NBC had been around in those days.

Meanwhile, famine had broken out in the land of the Hebrews, so his brothers came to Egypt to buy food. Guess whom they had to negotiate with? On a platter, as it were, Joseph was offered the chance to pay his brothers back, big-time. You can read the details for yourself in Genesis 41–46. I am intrigued by a small item in the account of the names Joseph had given his two children. Names had great significance for the Hebrews. Joseph named his firstborn, Manasseh, *"because God has made me forget all my trouble and all my father's household"* (41:51 NIV, emphasis added). Not forget most, but *all* his troubles. I would, at least, have kept a couple of mementos for my scrapbook. Joseph called his second son, Ephraim, *"because God has made me fruitful in the land of my suffering"* (41:52 NIV, emphasis added).

What a message of contrast! Ephraim: "God has made me fruitful in the land of my suffering." A whole string of unexplainables had happened to a young man named Joseph. How this Hebrew must have suffered. I suspect that you haven't forgotten all your troubles or the individuals

49

responsible. Has God—no, have you allowed God—to make *you* "fruitful in the land of your sufferings"?

There are three tenets of shame, according to the Twelve-Step theory:

1. I am worthless and unacceptable to God, myself, and others.
2. Others will abandon [hurt] me. I must meet my own needs. [Take care of #1]
3. Life will never get better, and I am helpless to change it.[4]

Are you constantly rehearsing number 3: "Life will never get better! I am helpless to change it"? Or are you inviting God to make you fruitful? Without grace you end up with desolation.

Bill Huebsch summarized the issue in *A Spirituality of Wholeness*, when he wrote:

This whole, simple process
    of naming our experiences in life,
    of coming to the edge,
    of facing the ultimate questions,
    of choosing to turn back or go beyond
    is something we often face alone.
But for those who choose to move beyond
    for these who choose to die to self,
    this journey
        to the heart of the Lord
        will not be traveled alone.
And this is our point here:
    we are graced,
    everyone is graced,
    empowered, in other words,
    to move beyond and be transformed.[5]

4

SINGLE AND BELONGING

What is the point of having a life if you didn't say something or do something that is going to survive after you're gone?" asked Pedro Almodovar, whose quotation has made its way to my refrigerator door. That question is summed up in the brief but shining life of a single adult named Jonathan Daniels.

During the sixties, according to Charles W. Eagles of the University of Mississippi, "Americans were still willing to commit themselves to causes larger than themselves." They were not content with the excuse, "I am only one person." As a student at Episcopal Theological Seminary, his fieldwork in an urban parish introduced Jon to "the enormous social problems involving race and poverty" and gave him occasion to consider how the gospel might affect communities suffering from poverty and powerlessness. In March 1965, Jon, with other seminarians, went to Alabama to join Dr. Martin Luther King, Jr., in a voting rights campaign. When the march was over, many "outside agitators," as they were labeled, returned to their classrooms, parishes, and jobs in the North. Jon returned to Alabama, noting, "I could not stand by in benevolent dispassion any longer" and not "stand beside the weak and . . . support their protests." The dominant white population said, "Yankee boy, you don't *belong* here! Go back up North where you belong! (and a few unprintable suggestions). This is a Southern problem."

No, Jon Daniels countered, racism is a spiritual problem. He refused to leave.

On August 20, 1965, in Hayneville, Alabama, that refusal cost him his life. Although Tom Coleman, his murderer, was acquitted, blacks redoubled their efforts to win their equal rights. In many ways, this New Englander did not belong in the South; but after ministry in the South he did not belong in the North either.

This twenty-six-year-old single adult, according to Dr. Eagles, was "compelled only by his faith to live according to the teachings of Christian love and by an existential need to act."[1]

Jon Daniels belongs to a cadre of courageous single adults who have done something that has survived their lives.

Where do you belong?

AMERICANS ARE BELONGERS

Over thirty thousand nationally recognized organizations exist in this country; more are organized weekly.

Some people belong to service clubs: Rotary, Lions, Kiwanis, Jaycees, Sertoma, Optimist.

Some belong passionately to political parties: Democratic, Republican, Libertarian.

Some belong to fraternal organizations: Elks, Moose, Masons, Eastern Star, Knights of Columbus.

Some belong to unions: UAW, Teamsters, IGW, ICW.

Some belong to professional organizations: NEA, ABA, APA, AMA.

Some belong to special interest groups: NRA, Urban League, NGO, AAA, American Legion, VFW, Junior League, AARP, YMCA, or YWCA.

Then there are the churches that Americans belong to: denominations (more than one hundred different varieties of Baptists alone), independents, inter- and nondenominationals.

Clearly, Americans are joiners and belong to many organizations—if you don't believe that just read through the obituaries. It's amazing how a group of people can gather around a particular need and suddenly you have a movement.

- When Ethel Andrus, a single adult, retired from teaching public school, she discovered there were a lot of poor retired school teachers. She organized the American Association of Retired Persons or AARP, one of the strongest lobby groups in this country.
- When Flora Adams Darling, a single adult, realized the need for more patriotism among children, the result was the Daughters of the American Revolution, the DAR.[2]

As early as 1835, Alexis de Tocqueville observed, "If [Americans] want to proclaim a truth or promulgate some feeling by the encouragement of a great example, they form an association. . . . I have come across several types of associations in America of which, I confess, I had not previously the slightest conception."[3]

Maybe it is only a matter of time until a National Association of Reluctantly Single Persons (NARSP) is formed, complete with chapters, newsletters, lobbyists, and an annual convention.

Belonging Is an Early Lesson to Be Learned

The first place we belong is in a family. Some families make it very easy and comfortable and safe and secure to belong. In other families, you wouldn't close both eyes during a mealtime blessing, if there is one.

Some of us know what it is to be adopted.

Some of us know what it is to be disinherited.

Some of us know what it is to be treated as second class at Christmas and holidays.

If you had an older brother or sister you probably heard at least once that classic line, "Two's company and three's a crowd! Scram!" Some of us had to baby-sit a younger brother or sister and at times were very annoyed. Who can forget the power of the cliques in our schools, churches, or neighborhoods with their subtle message, "You don't belong!"

The second place we belong is to an educational organization, a school. I still remember when Jefferson County Public Schools in Kentucky went to a tract program: S (Superior), R (Regular), and U (Underachievers). I wasn't in the top academic group, and it was always clear that a certain class was made up of Ss. I remember feeling left out, embarrassed. But not as much as those who were reassigned to the group early in the school year because they couldn't keep up with the pace.

Carson McCullers captured this mood in her depiction of a twelve-year-old named Frankie, in *The Member of the Wedding*. "It happened that green and crazy summer when Frankie was twelve years old. This was the summer when for a long time she had not been a member. She belonged to no club and was a member of nothing in the world. Frankie had become an unjoined person."[4] A lot of single adults today feel like "unjoined" persons.

All of us have, at some point, heard these words of barbed rejection: *You don't belong!* All of us have experienced their sting.

Cultural Rejection

In the early 1830s, Dorothea had one of the greatest literary talents in Boston. By age twenty-seven she had written several books and taught school, yet she could not break into that inner elite circle in Boston society. She was not invited to tea at William Ellery Channing's home with Emerson, Holmes, Longfellow, or Alcott. Nor was she invited to the select literary gatherings at Elizabeth Peabody's Bookshop on West Street. Although brilliant, she didn't belong.

But Dorothea Dix used that rejection to reach out to others who didn't belong: the mentally ill, generally housed in public jails due to the prevailing attitude of "out of sight, out of mind." Dorothea became "God's missionary to the insane." When she began her campaign for public recognition of the need for compassionate care in 1843, there were only 13 mental health facilities; by 1880, after years of dedicated and persistent lobbying, the number had reached 123.[5]

A single adult, Dorothea Dix, made a difference!

Racial Belonging

Ideas on belonging can be challenged, as evidenced by the change in racial attitudes in this nation. Mary, one of thirteen children in a sharecropper's family, was the only child in the family to go to school. Eventually, Mary became the first black to graduate from Moody Bible Institute. However, when she applied for mission service in Africa she was rejected. Was Mary unqualified? No, she was black. She didn't belong, the Presbyterian Board of Missions said, in foreign missions. That "no" was "the greatest disappointment in my life," Mary later explained. Reluctantly she had to admit, "My life work lay not in Africa but in my own country" and in the White House.[6]

Mary Bethune eventually founded a school for poor black children, buying the city garbage dump in Daytona Beach, Florida. The KKK said she didn't belong and that black children should not be educated! Mary stood her ground, and across the years Bethune-Cookman College has educated thousands of Americans.

A single adult, Mary Bethune, made a difference!

Spiritual Rejection

Sometimes, a church decides certain people do not fit in. Third Presbyterian Church in Charleston, South Carolina, decided in 1829, that a single adult, Angelina Grimke, did not belong after she stood in a church meeting and announced her intention to free her slaves. She was barred from fellowship for having "a rebellious spirit." Angelina Grimke used the rejection to help launch the abolitionist movement in this country.[7]

Countless single adults have been formally excommunicated or denied communion after being divorced, even when someone else made the decision and the church member merely inherited the consequences. Some churches insist that divorced individuals do not belong in ministry. While editing this chapter, my concentration was interrupted by a call from a minister in a very conservative denomination, who after a divorce asked, "Do I *still* belong in ministry?" His denomination loudly says "no."

Let me share a personal story. Several years ago, while I was speaking on the subject of divorce at a large single-adult conference in the Seattle Center, a note reached me at the podium:

> You are so wrong!
> I hope God can forgive you for the wrong steer you have given all these people. You pull Scripture out of context and put it down the way you want to interpret it to mean. This is supposed to be a *Christian* conference and you don't belong here!

How do you deal with feelings of not belonging?

Neighborhood Rejection

One reality that must be overcome is the residue of housing discrimination. Carole was told that she didn't belong in a certain Chicago neighborhood. Her "kind" should live elsewhere. Amazingly, that little girl didn't let the taunting get to her. It gave her an undergirding for the rough-and-tumble world of Chicago politics. When she was announced as a candidate for the U.S. Senate against a powerful incumbent—inspired by the courage of Anita Hill—people shook their heads: sacrificial lamb! Some racists said she didn't belong in the United States Senate! A majority of Illinois voters disagreed and elected her to the Senate, where she is breaking up the "good old boy" network that has so long governed that institution. Carole Moseley-Braun, a single parent at the time of her election, became the country's first black female senator.

She demonstrated that she would not play by the "good old boy's" rules when a Southern senator attempted to defend the patent of a design that included the Confederate flag. This freshman senator made the Senate stop and listen. Although the Senate had approved the flag's use 52–48, Moseley-Braun stood and through her tears and anger declared:

> On this issue there can be no consensus. It is an outrage. It is an insult. It is absolutely unacceptable to me and to millions of Americans, black or white, that we would put the imprimatur of the United States Senate on a symbol on this kind of idea.[8]

As word of the debate spread, senators returned to the chamber to listen, and ultimately the Senate voted to reverse itself. A few days later, in the Judiciary Committee, as one member attempted to grill Judge Ruth Bader Ginsburg, the Supreme Court nominee, again Senator

Moseley-Braun interrupted to point out to the senator that it was a new day. "This line of questioning I find to be personally offensive." It is "difficult to sit here as the only descendant of a slave in this committee, in this body, and hear" such a line of questioning.[9]

MANY SINGLE ADULTS HAVE A DEEP SENSE OF BEING "LEFT OUT"

Many reluctantly single adults feel left out in many of America's fast-growing family-focused churches. Some churches still have Christian education classes named, "Pairs and Spares" or token single-adult programs. The emphasis, however, is clear: If you want to be accepted around here, get married.

Two thousand years ago, the apostle Paul, a single adult, wrote, "There is no longer Jew or Greek, there is no longer slave or free, there is no longer male and female" (Gal. 3:28). Dare I add, *married or single*? Ironically, if Paul were alive today, he would not be allowed to freely minister in some congregations because of his naked ring finger. He would have to find a wife.

Yet, Paul declared, labels are meaningless to God. "*All* of you are one in Christ Jesus and . . . heirs according to the promise" (Gal. 3:28-29, emphasis added). Paul obviously meant that, but it is not true in every church in this land, especially in some that claim to be the most faithful interpreters of Scripture. Neither Jesus nor Paul would be enthusiastically welcomed since they were unmarried.

Listen to what Philomone Gates discovered after her husband died:

If you're like most people, most of your "friends" are business acquaintances and professional associates

58

rather than true friends. There's nothing wrong with that, but you may find that many of these relationships came into your life through your husband's business, and now that he's dead, they will disappear.[10]

Divorced individuals as well as widows and widowers understand the subtle but effective distancing:

My place in the world was also drastically altered. People who had been friendly in the past were now awkward around me. The first time I went to the mailroom at the university, some of my colleagues were gathered around, passing the time and chatting. I walked in and everything changed. The easy conversation turned to dead silence. The joviality turned to haste to get out of the room. Within seconds everyone was gone![11]

Church folk may be almost hoarse from singing "Getting Used to the Family of God," but they will walk right past you in the foyer of the church without speaking, let alone inviting you to join them for pie and coffee. Single adults are seldom if ever invited to join in the couple-dominated socializing in the church—after all, you know, that's how "things" get started. You might as well have S-I-N-G-L-E or W-I-D-O-W-E-D or D-I-V-O-R-C-E-D branded on your forehead. Some churches might as well put up signs:

SINGLE ADULTS NOT WELCOME HERE!
DIVORCÉES NOT WELCOME HERE!
MIDDLE-AGED SINGLE ADULTS NOT WELCOME HERE!
SINGLE PARENTS NOT WELCOME HERE!

Karen experienced this. Her husband was a pastor. While she was in labor with their second son, her husband scolded, "Would you hurry up and have this baby! There are people who need me!" The Reverend Sensitivity. Eventually, they divorced. Divorced with two children, her denomination might as well have said, "Depart from us, Karen, we never knew you!"

Karen read a book I had written about divorce and wrote me a long, troubling letter about how single mothers *and their children* were treated in churches; how they didn't belong in family-centric congregations. She described some of the ways she and her two boys had been made to feel that they did not belong.

I wrote Karen, "Try X church in your town. They will welcome you."

She wrote back, "Don't they handle snakes?"

I sent a postcard: "They don't expect first-timers to do that."

The pastor of the church I had recommended later shared how he met Karen and the boys. About ten minutes into the Sunday evening service, a young mother with two small boys would slip into a back pew only to disappear during the closing prayer. Week after week: 6:10 arrival, 6:59 departure. Her punctuality drove this pastor nuts!

One night he decided to pray the benediction in the back of the church. While he was praying she tried to slip by but he grabbed her arm and said, "Wait a minute! I want to talk to you! Why do you come so punctually at 6:10 but always leave before any of our folks can meet you?"

She looked down. "I'm not sure you would want me here. If you knew about . . . "

"Lady," the pastor interrupted, "this is God's house! Everyone's welcome *here*."

"Well, that's what Harold Ivan said, but I just can't risk any more rejection."

"Please," said the pastor, "let us get to know you."

In many congregations, single adults are simply ignored. They are welcomed to worship and make financial

60

contributions, but are not actively included in social gatherings in the life of the congregation. Some are too polite to make a scene.

CHURCH GROWTH AND BELONGING

Too many churches, in order to chase the current fixation with church-growth principles (a slightly spiritualized form of marketing), have turned family from an *ideal* into an idol! Family values become the litmus test to belonging. Single-parent family? Oops—you'll feel more comfortable elsewhere. Single adult? You must be either gay or unstable.

A cadre of church growth "experts" travel the corridors of Christendom extolling the virtues of *homogeneous* family-oriented congregations as the fastest way to grow toward "success." Many have token, anemic single-adult groups. What they want is the typical suburban family: mother *and* father, 2.3 children, and a dog named Spot. Janet Fishburn, Professor of Teaching Ministry at Drew University, disagrees with the "pro-family" marketing strategy of so many churches:

> The price of uncritical commitment to "the family pew"
> is the perpetuation of attitudes that will make anyone
> who is the "wrong" color, class, or sexual orientation
> feel excluded. Under the surface of many "successful"
> congregations lurk the stereotypes and prejudices (well
> nourished) now ruled unacceptable in civil courts.[12]

Fishburn concludes, "Membership in a church 'family' can become idolatrous if a congregation includes only people who are comfortable with one another."[13]

Admittedly, there are other arenas in which people are made to feel that they do not belong because they are unmarried; but only the church claims to be the body of Christ. A woman testifies before a congressional committee. One senior senator mumbles, "Aren't you pretty! I bet you're married. And if you aren't, that's a shame!"[14] That was his way of saying, You don't belong here before this committee. Your testimony doesn't count for much to me.

"Tell Us About Your Family"

How many times has someone used that tired old cliché to jump-start a conversation: "Tell us about your family"?

What happened when you answered, "I'm not married"?

WHAM! You can see it in their eyes: "That's odd . . . you look old enough to be married."

I now carry pictures to answer that question. "Oh, let me show you my pride and joy." I pull out a snapshot of bottles of Pride and Joy. About the only response I get from married folk is, "Very funny."

In one too many settings the message is, "If you aren't married there is something wrong with you."

Single in My World

A nice white Gentile moved into an old Jewish neighborhood in Kansas City. The matriarch of the neighborhood stood on the sidewalk, watching him move in.

"And how many kids are you bringing into the neighborhood to disturb the peaceful tranquillity?" she demanded.

"None," I answered.

"Such a shame—these career women who don't want children!" Her frown quickly led me to interrupt, "Oh, I'm not married."

"There's one of those that lives up the block," she said, gesturing with her head. After a moment, "But maybe you are a smart Gentile boy. With this house you'll get a better wife." I suspect what she was really thinking was, "There goes the neighborhood!"

I remember being an executive in my former denomination and having to call a pastor about some disturbing behavior by a single adult who belonged to his church. After I had shared a few initial details, he interrupted, "They're all crazy, Harold Ivan. That's why they are single!"

"Pastor X," I interrupted, "do you know that I am single?"

"Well," he sputtered, "I don't mean every last one of them—but the good majority of them. If they were normal they would be married by now."

The church can hint so subtly, "You . . . do not . . . belong."

Father's Day

I still remember my first Father's Day as a single adult. "Now we want all the fathers," our minister directed, "to come up to the choir loft. We're going to have an all-father's choir." I was the only adult male left seated in the congregation. That Sunday I felt I didn't belong.

Single women—as well as married women who can't conceive—understand this feeling every Mother's Day. What is it like as a single woman in your church that Sunday? Do you feel left out? Are you reminded in a dozen little ways that you don't belong?

Belonging and the Family

The Genesis 2:18 Syndrome

It goes back to a common misinterpretation of Genesis 2:18, "It is not good that the man should be alone." So many church folk think we'd be in la-la land if only everyone were married.

Some of us have an Aunt Ethel or Uncle Earl—God love 'em—who always know what to say to light our sparklers at family gatherings! At Thanksgiving Uncle Earl looks across what's left of the turkey, pats his belly and grins, "Well! Well! Well! Another year has gone by and you are *still* single! What exactly is your problem?"

Ever experienced that little scenario?

One single friend contends, "Stupid questions deserve stupid answers—especially if you aren't in the will."

"Uncle Earl," you respond, pausing to capture the attention around the table, "I've been looking at your marriage and thought I could do a lot better by waiting!"

Be sure you have the Heimlich maneuver handy—you may need it.

Uncle Earl declares, "Bless God, I just believe Genesis 2:18: 'It is not good for man to be alone.' "

That Scripture does not mean everybody ought to get married. Because not everyone is ready for the responsibilities and duties and obligations and sacrifices that modern marriage requires.

The New Testament and Family

In recent years, Christians have relied more on a narrow cultural understanding of marriage and family rather than a distinctive New Testament viewpoint. But the New Testament doesn't talk about a nuclear family. The Apostle Paul didn't have the foggiest idea about the composition of a nuclear family. In fact, Jesus said, without blinking an eye, that anyone who loved family more than him was not worthy of the kingdom. Jesus demanded, "Who are my mother and brothers?" and made it clear that family in his view was not biological but spiritual, "Whoever does the will of God is my brother and sister and mother" (Mark 3:35).

Jesus understood well the dysfunctional family. Mark reported occasions when Jesus was so busy that he did not have time to eat. "When his family heard about this, they went to take charge of him, for they said, '*He is out of his mind*'" (Mark 3:21 NIV). Have you ever heard a sermon on that Scripture? Jesus' family thought he was crazy! They wanted to take "charge" of a thirty-year-old man as if he were a child.

Definitely, the New Testament does not emphasize the biological, nuclear, suburban family. It describes a radically more expansive and inclusive concept called "the family of God" or "the household of faith" (Gal. 6:10)! One reason the early church grew so rapidly was that they *included* rather than excluded.

The nuclear family has existed about forty-plus years in this country, but the concept has a stranglehold on the thinking of some religious leaders.

The major barrier to single adult ministry is that too many leaders have allowed their attitudes about family composition to be shaped by longings for some fantasy of family in previous historical time periods rather than reality.

The Jewish Family in Jesus' Day

The Jewish attitude on families in Jesus' day could be summarized:

- *Everyone* had to get married.
- *Everyone* had to have children.
- If your current wife couldn't give you a child—preferably male—get a wife who could!
- To divorce: clap your hands three times and say: "I divorce you! I divorce you! I divorce you!" The woman ended up a prostitute because that was the only way she could survive financially in a predominantly pro-family culture.
- The worst thing that could happen to a woman was to be barren.

Even a casual reading of the Old Testament discloses that many women suffered enormously under the Jewish "pro-family" traditions and were made to feel that they did not belong. One barren woman named Hannah was harassed mercilessly by her husband's culturally mandated and very fertile second wife! Hannah, in acute emotional distress, was observed praying in the Tabernacle of Meeting and was confronted by the prophet Eli, who accused her of being drunk! Hannah answered, "No, my lord, I am a woman deeply troubled. . . . I have been pouring out my soul before the LORD. . . . I have been speaking out of my great anxiety and vexation" (1 Sam. 1:15-16).

Some reluctantly single adults have voiced similar words and felt the same anguish. How many times have you pleaded with God for someone to love? For God to nudge the Right One in your direction?

A second Old Testament story underscores the point of belonging.

Abram had complained to God, "What good are all your blessings when I have no heir?" (Gen. 15:2 para-phrase). I've got a wife, a zillion sheep and cattle—but I have no son to inherit all that I own. Who was at fault?

"Now Sarai, Abram's wife, had borne him no children" (Gen. 16:1 NIV).

She may have been a wonderful wife but, from a Jewish perspective, Sarai was flawed because she had not given Abram a son! "But she had an Egyptian maidservant named Hagar, so she [Sarai] said to Abram, 'The LORD has kept me from having children. Go, sleep with my maid-servant; perhaps I can build a family through her' " (Gen. 16:2 NIV).

Sarai, to say the least, was not content to wait any longer for a tardy God—for God's timing. She wanted a family *now*. Sarai was about as impatient for a child as some single adults are for marriage today. God had promised Abram he would have descendants as numerous as the stars, which meant that God would have taken care of the details—in *his* time, in *his* way. But Sarai sat down in the director's chair and rewrote the scene. "Abram agreed . . . . He slept with Hagar, and she conceived. When she knew that she was pregnant, she began to despise her mistress." Poor Abram, was torn between the two women. "Then Sarai said to Abram: 'You are responsible for the wrong I am suffering. I put my servant in your arms. . . . She despises me' " (Gen. 16:5, NIV). This is all your fault! Abram must have stuttered, "Me? This was your big idea!" The tension between the two women turned nasty. "Then Sarai mistreated Hagar; so she fled" (Gen. 16:6 NIV).

Tough position for a single adult to be put into, huh? Talk about not belonging. Hagar, a maid, an Egyptian, had only a servant's sense of belonging, tenuous at best. Few rights, no one to protect her. But God had plans for this single adult—just like he has plans monogrammed with our initials. "The angel of the LORD found Hagar near a spring in the desert . . . . And he said, 'Hagar, servant of Sarai, where have you come from, and where are you going?' " (Gen. 16:1-8 NIV).

Whew! A confrontational bull's-eye. Next time you think God doesn't know what's going on in your desert, remember Hagar. God not only knew where she was, he also knew who she was and her employer.

QUESTIONS THAT DESERVE ANSWERS

These questions zing down through four thousand years to confront single adults: *"Where have you come from? Where are you going?"*

Time out! Put this book down and reflect on your answers to those two questions:

1. Where have you *come from*?
2. Where are you *going*?

Your answers are crucial not merely to survive as a reluctant single adult, but also to thrive in spite of your reluctance to be single.

Where have you come from? Divorce? Widowhood? Never married? Swinging-single life-style? Most readers, I assume, are not fresh from a convent. Most of us have been around the track a few laps. Too many of us have scars and bruises and fears and doubts and inadequacies. Our past does color our present, but only with our permission.

Where are you headed? Will the rest of your single season be like what you have experienced so far? You moan, "I hope not!"

To her credit, Hagar answers the angel straightfor-wardly, "I'm running away from my mistress, Sarai" (Gen. 16:8 NIV).

What we'd like to read in this account is compassion by the angel. "Hey girl, head over to . . . there's a real short-age of maids over there. They'll treat you better. Working conditions will be much better."

No. Instead, the angel says, "Go back to your mistress and submit to her" (Gen. 16:9 NIV).

Submit? Did you say *submit*?

That's definitely not what Hagar wanted to hear. That's definitely *not* what I want to hear. But before Hagar could protest, the angel added, "I will so increase your descen-dants that they will be too numerous to count" (Gen. 16:10 NIV).

Catch that phrase: *your descendants*. Not just Abram's descendants would be too numerous to count, but God also promised to multiply Hagar's descendants.

But that's not all. The angel confirmed that indeed Hagar was pregnant, so the promise was already unfold-ing. Then the angel added a remarkable footnote:

"For the LORD has heard of your misery" (Gen. 16:11 NIV).

Amazing! God the eternal parent has heard the cries of one mistreated pregnant Egyptian maid in the desert!

YOUR DESERT

Perhaps as you read this, you're in a desert. You hate being single.

Desert: hot, ugly—so different from that split-level four-bedroomer you had when you were married. So different from your dorm room or your accommodations when you lived with your parents. So different from your well-worn dreams, fantasies, and expectations.

Guess what? God's words to Hagar, I believe, could be God's words to you. "The Lord has heard of *your* misery." The Lord knows that you are in the dry, hot, barren desert called singleness and that you long for a lush, green pasture called marriage.

The timing I cannot promise. But the Lord has heard. Because he is a loving God, he will work for your good on his timetable. *His* timetable.

That could mean more desert. You may have to go back and submit to this day-to-day routine of singleness. You may have to experience some more feelings of not belonging. You too have to go back. Oh! You protest. I don't belong in the land of singleness! I only want a visa for a short stay, not citizenship.

I'm tired of being "positively" single!

I'm tired of being reluctantly single!

I'm tired of not belonging!

I'm tired of singles' conferences and singles' groups and the personals and singles' nights at the Winn-Dixie!

First you have to answer "Where have you come from?" before you can answer "Where are you going?"

WHEN SUSANNAH'S "BELONGING" BEGAN

An famed incident in Texas history illustrates the point. We have heard a great deal about the men of the Alamo—legends in American history. But many have forgotten or have never known of the great woman of the Alamo, Susannah A. Dickerson, wife of Captain Almeron Dickerson.

Susannah and her fifteen-month-old daughter, Angelina, were present during the entire siege and spent most of the time in the chapel. At one point, her husband of six years rushed to the frightened twenty-one-year-old and gasped, "Great God, Sue, the Mexicans are inside our walls! All is lost! If they spare you, save my child." Even the chapel was not spared death; she watched Jacob Walker shot and bayonetted a few feet from her and her child. Susannah was wounded in the calf by gunshot.[15]

The great Mexican general, Santa Anna, interviewed her, offering to take her and her daughter back to Mexico; the little one would be raised by the general as a princess. Susannah promptly refused. So he gave her two pecos and a blanket and sent her away.

Eventually, Susannah was the person to describe the slaughter at the Alamo to General Houston and to convey Santa Anna's threat: Every Texan in rebellion would meet the same fate—no survivors!

According to historian Jeff Long, once that information was conveyed, "Susannah was essentially discarded. The assumption was that someone would care for her." A bad assumption. The next two decades could be described as hell for the heroine; neither she nor her daughter ever received a penny of financial assistance from Texas, even though they were at times destitute.

Deeply traumatized by the Alamo violence (seeing nearly every man she knew in Texas executed by the Mexicans), Susannah became a virtual model of self-

destruction, marrying four times and sinking into nym-
phomania and prostitution in the city named for Sam
Houston. Her second husband beat her until she miscar-
ried. (Susannah gained one of the first divorces granted in
Texas.) Husband three died of 'digestive fever,' a euphe-
mism for alcoholism. Husband four divorced her on
grounds of adultery (and residing in a house of ill fame).

She also had to watch her daughter divorce, go into
prostitution, and—finally die a horrible death with a hem-
orraging uterus.

Susannah Dickerson was shunned by polite Texas society, although occasionally she was asked to testify in favor
of grants to heirs of Alamo survivors. Then an invitation
came. Rufus Burlinson, pastor of First Baptist Church of
Houston, was conducting a revival and canvassed the
neighborhood to find nonmembers. He invited Susannah
to the revival; she declined, stating that she doubted she
would be welcomed by the good Christian folks. "Our
church is open to you," Burlinson retorted. He asked her
her name.

"Susannah Dickerson" she replied softly.

"*The* Susannah Dickerson?" the astonished pastor
asked. She nodded. "You are welcome at the First Baptist
Church anytime."

During that revival, she heard such grace preached that
it became clear to her that despite her soiled past, she could
belong to God's kingdom. In that revival, Susannah Dickerson gave her life to Christ and surrendered what even
the pastor called "a great bundle of untamed passions."
Historian Long concludes his discussion of her by noting,
"Just so, after many years of suffering, the whore Susannah regained her innocence."[16] She became an outstand-
ing member of the church.

Where are you coming from? Where are you going?
Where do you belong?

Always remember: You belong to God!

5

SINGLE AND RELEVANT

Y ou can't miss it!" That's what the man at the cemetery office had told me when I asked the location of a particular grave. He was right. A large bronze marker identified the grave of a baby boomer who had attained incredible political power. Many believed his strategy had been responsible for a president's election. This boomer had it all: friends in high places, family, high income, prestige, and one other thing— cancer. He had belonged to an elite cadre of movers and shakers, a handful of individuals who had decided what the priorities of this nation would be. Now, the words in the bronze captured my imagination:

> I do not choose to be a common man.
> It is my right to be uncommon.
> I prefer the challenges
>   of life to guaranteed security;
> The thrill of fulfillment to the
>   stale calm of utopia.
> I will never cower before any master,
>   save my God.

My visit to Lee Atwater's grave in Columbia, South Carolina, left an incredible impression on me. Those words "I do not choose to be a common man" remained long after the visit. Throughout history, God has raised up individuals to respond to the Spirit's initiatives, particularly in matters of injustice. God simply does not say, "I'd better take care of this . . ." and whoom! Rather, God finds one of his children, gifted, capable, courageous, obedient, and through the Spirit, brings that individual to an awareness that there is a problem that needs to be confronted, an injustice to be righted.

Simply, God calls down through the centuries and says today, "Take me seriously." If single adults would take God seriously, many of the issues, problems, difficulties, and heartaches of humanity could be resolved.

I have a postcard above my word processor that reads, "I will act as though what I do makes a difference," which the calligrapher attributes to philosopher William James. After reading biographical material on over a thousand single adults in the professions, government, churches, schools, business, and social movements, I am convinced that one person *can* make a difference. This principle has been demonstrated in the lives and actions of single adults I have highlighted in this book—and will be demonstrated in the lives of some who read it.

HENRY MARTYN

This principle is demonstrated in the life of a reluctant single, Henry Martyn. Henry had established himself as a brilliant scholar at Cambridge University in the early 1800s. One day, while reading the biography of another single adult, David Brainerd, missionary and justice advocate among Native Americans, Martyn closed the book and prayed, "Here I am, Lord. Send me to the ends of the earth; send me to the rough, the savage pagans of the wilderness."

73

He volunteered as a candidate for India to the Church Missionary Society and was influenced by the evangelical leader of England, Charles Simeon, also a single adult. Romance complicated the decision because Henry had fallen in love with Lydia Grenfell. The mission board encouraged the relationship, saying, "If the missionary's wife is worthy of her calling, she *doubles* his usefulness," and models to a pagan world the powerful witness of a Christian marriage.[1]

Lydia, however, had broken her engagement to a Samuel John, and because of the value placed on engagement in those days, she did not feel free to marry Henry until her former fiancé married. At times, Martyn described his love for Lydia and his hunger for mission service as "a deadly rivalry." He struggled with his calling: could he go to India without her? At one point, he thought he had made the decision but journaled, "but in a moment my heart had wandered to the beloved idol. I went to bed in great pain, yet still superior to my enemy; but in dreams her image returned, and I awoke in the night, with my mind full of her."[2] Many reluctantly single adults fully understand Martyn's phrase, "I awoke in the night, with my mind full of her [him]."

Finally, through great pain, he concluded, "If God made me, and wills my happiness, as I do not doubt, then He is providing for my good by separating me from her." His journal depicts their last meeting, Lydia, her father, and Martyn walking along the coast. Henry was distracted. "Now, thought I, here am I in the presence of God, and my idol." His last sentence that day is telling, "Parted with Lydia, perhaps forever in this life, with a sort of uncertain pain, which I knew would increase to greater violence."[3] Who said that only the divorced or widowed know pain?

During the next seven years, Martyn traveled to India, Persia, and Arabia and translated the Bible into Arabic, Persian, and Hindustani. He died en route to Constantinople on October 16, 1812, and was buried in an unmarked grave alongside the road. The caravaners had no idea who he was. From his journal one final notation:

> I am born for God only. Christ is nearer to me than father or mother or sister—a nearer relative, a more intimate friend; and I rejoice to follow Him and to love him.[4]

Recognition of his greatness came long after his death; his remarkable translation experience not only opened the Muslim world to Christianity but also to commerce with the West. Henry Martyn was a single adult who lived as though what he did made a difference.

WHO IS "THE GREATEST?"

Do you remember Muhammad Ali boldly proclaiming, "I am the greatest!!!" Three-time world heavyweight boxing champion, Olympic gold-medalist, a master with words as well as his fists. Who could forget his boast, "Float like a butterfly, sting like a bee!"? Still, Ali's boasting "I am the greatest!" annoyed even some of his most devout fans.

The issue of "the greatest" plagued the disciples and apparently was an ongoing debate during their off hours. Matthew reported that they "came to Jesus and asked, 'Who is the greatest in the kingdom of heaven?'" (Matt. 18:1). I suspect that, among themselves, they had a tentative ranking and were seeking confirmation from Jesus.

To answer that question, Jesus summoned a child and said, "Unless you change and become like children, you will never enter the kingdom of heaven" (v. 3). The disciples, unfortunately, didn't follow his logic. Two chapters later, Matthew reports a remarkable episode of jockeying for position.

The mother of James and John came to Jesus with her two sons, "and kneeling before him, she asked a favor of him" (Matt. 20:20).

Jesus asked what she wanted. This must have silenced the group and added dramatic flair. "Declare that these two sons of mine will sit, one at your right hand and one at your left, in your kingdom" (Matt. 20:21).

Now, someone would get those positions. It is not as if she is asking Jesus to create a position for her boys. And James and John were good boys. However, Momma is asking for a lot more. Johnson paraphrases her request to read, "Permit my two sons to have places of recognition and authority," or, in other words, "Put my two boys at the head of the line."[5]

To her credit, she doesn't hint around or mince words. She apparently didn't "butter up" Jesus; no fresh baked goods or new garment. Clearly, her sons, John and James, were no strangers to Jesus. Indeed, no one was closer to Jesus than John. Five times the Scriptures report that Jesus loved John (John 13:23; 19:26; 20:02, 21:7, 20), passages seldom preached because they make us uncomfortable. We can deal with Jesus loving everyone but not specific individuals.

On the strength of their earthly relationship, we can almost expect Jesus to say, "You got it. Anything else I can do for you while I am in the giving mood?" Hardly. Jesus answered, no doubt aware that the disciples were closely listening, "Not one of you [the one asking; the ones who perhaps put Momma up to asking; the ones who craved the position but were not bold enough to seek it] knows what you are asking." Oh, but they did. They simply wanted to be recognized as Jesus' right-hand and left-hand men. Jesus ignored the mother to confront the two volunteers. "Are you able to drink the cup that I am about to drink?" (Matt. 20:22).

Surely Momma had anticipated such a question and had rehearsed the boys. Without any hesitation, James and John answered, "Yes, we are!" Grins probably stretched across their faces and Momma beamed like a proud Jewish parent. "Oh, yes. Definitely, yes!"

Jesus replied, "You will indeed drink my cup!" although, at this point, none of the trio realized that *cup* meant sacrifice or death. Jesus further clarified his response, "to sit at my right hand and at my left, this is not mine to grant, but it is for those for whom it has been prepared by my Father" (Matt. 20:23).

Momma and her two boys now had to deal with some annoyed eavesdroppers, perhaps even angry with the two brothers, if not with Momma as well. Discussions about pecking order and greatness generally imply that if there's someone at the top of the list, someone has to be at the bottom. Momma fades into the sunset; James and John take a low profile until the next time the subject comes up. Jesus seized this teachable moment and said, "You know that the rulers of the Gentiles lord it over them, and their great ones are tyrants over them. It will not be so among you." I see Jesus pausing, his eyes locked on John and James "but whoever wishes to be great among you must be your servant, and whoever wishes to be first among you must be your slave; just as the Son of Man came not to be served but to serve, and to give his life a ransom for many" (Matt. 20:25-28).

The disciples still didn't get it. On another occasion, in Capernaum, Jesus asked them, "What were you arguing about on the way?" (Mark 9:33). But they would not answer, probably mumbling like schoolboys, "Oh . . . nothing." But Jesus knew what they had been arguing about and responded, "Whoever wants to be first must be last of all and servant of all" (Mark 9:35).

Interestingly, Jesus did not fault them for wanting to occupy a place of honor—that's just human nature. But he did say that the route to the place of honor is servanthood.

To illustrate his point, Jesus had a child stand near him. The object lesson was lost on the Twelve, as it is often lost on us. In Jesus' day, children were insignificant, except to someone as sensitive as Jesus.

I prefer Mark's account of Jesus questioning John and James: "You do not know what you are asking" (10:38). That is still true for single adults. We ask—in verbalized and unspoken prayers—for some of the most outlandish things.

Jesus' words still resound: whoever wants to become great among you must be a servant. When Jesus returned to his hometown from the wilderness temptation, he stood in the synagogue on the sabbath. Clearly here he was known as Joseph and Mary's boy. Jesus said

"The Spirit of the Lord is upon me,
    because he has anointed me
        to bring good news to the poor.
He has sent me to proclaim release to the captives
    and recovery of sight to the blind,
        to let the oppressed go free,
to proclaim the year of the Lord's favor."
                                        (Luke 4:18-19)

WHAT DO YOU WANT ME TO DO FOR YOU?

This was the agenda of a servant, of a slave, at least from Jesus' perspective. But let's slip back to Matthew's account. Interestingly, Jesus' encounter with the two volunteers for greatness and their mother is followed by an encounter with two blind men who had been told, "Shut up!" by the crowds around Jesus. However, they would not be hushed. They shouted "even louder." Jesus asked them, as he had the mother of James and John, "What do you want me to do for you?"

"Lord," they replied, "we want to see!"

Both of these stories, I think, are about blindness: one spiritual (James, John, and Momma) and the other physical (two blind men). Jesus' response, however, was specific. In the second instance, he "felt sorry for them and touched their eyes" and healed them, while in the first instance he may have felt sorry for the trio after the other disciples got through with them.

Two thousand years after this incident, Jesus asks reluctantly single adults the same question, "What do you want me to do for you?"

Most singles respond, "Give me a mate! And it would be great if he/she met the following physiological and economic specifications . . ." How many of us come to Jesus just like an exuberant child anxious to hop up on Santa's knee with a long Christmas wish list?

What would happen if we asked, as some single adults have done,

- Lord, help me to be relevant.
- Lord, help me act as though what I do makes a difference!
- Lord, help me recognize the Spirit's initiative in my life.
- Lord, help me not to waste these days of my life as a single adult.

Some single adults have dared to ask just that. Some have dared to risk it all with little evidence of a dividend. They have been jeered, denounced, rejected, ridiculed, and threatened. But their names and contributions cannot be ignored. Let's examine some relevant and reluctantly single adults.

SINGLES WHO MADE A DIFFERENCE

Mary Bartelme, Never Married

In 1923, Ilinois women had had the vote for three years when a young energetic "maiden" (in that day's vernacular) decided to run for Circuit Court Judge in Chicago. "A woman? Impossible!" the legal community scoffed. However, she had more qualifications than any male candidate: a graduate of Northwestern University Law School, public guardian for sixteen years, and assistant in Juvenile Court for ten years. Besides, this particular court often dealt with "wayward girls"; what a natural place for a woman to serve.

Bartelme's campaign was a tough one, and she had to endure a long grueling election night before the results were in. When she was declared the winner Mary exclaimed, "I knew it! I knew a woman could win." Soon she had a host of in-house supporters: lawyers, social workers, and politicians. Her philosophy was simple: "There are no bad children. There are confused, neglected, love-starved and resentful children, and what they need most I try to give them—understanding and a fresh start in the right direction."[6]

Judge Bartelme established new procedures to make the courtroom more humane. She often cleared the courtroom of the curious—particularly males—so that the girls' testimony would be more forthcoming. Because she disliked placing children in jail, Mary established homes where the girls could be "helped, encouraged, corrected but not 'reformed.' " To demonstrate her commitment to this judicial philosophy, she turned her own three-story home into a group home. Eventually, her facilities would be called "Mary Clubs" in her honor and were financed through contributions from private citizens.

Many of these young girls were troubled, not trouble-some. Some were the innocent victims of divorce or the loss of parents. As early as 1929, Judge Bartelme lamented, "The companionship of the home is no longer what it ought to be."

Jury duty in Mary's courtroom could be expensive. Many jurors, after listening to the testimony, opened their hearts and their pocketbooks. Tears were so common in her courtroom, in the eyes of jurors as well as young girls, that Mary kept a large supply of handkerchiefs for distribution.

Eventually, Judge Bartelme gained the nickname "Suitcase Mary" for her habit of supplying new clothes, nightwear, and necessities for the needy girls as they prepared to "graduate" from the Mary Club. More than one surprised young girl opened the suitcase and asked, "Is all this really mine?" Judge Bartelme said, "I believe that the young girls of Chicago and all Cook County are entitled to at least one judge who can deal with them in terms of real sympathy and understanding rather than in terms of legal lore and technicalities."[7]

In her years as a public servant in the judicial system, Mary Bartelme gave many girls a second or even third chance; few ever abused her generosity. One author noted, "As a judge . . . Bartelme had no grand scheme, no magnificent vision, other than wishing—and working hard—to provide a normal home for as many poor and friendless girls as possible."[8]

Mary Bartelme, a single adult, was relevant.

John Rowland/Henry Stanley, Single Adult

If John Rowland were alive today, Oprah, Geraldo, Phil Donahue, and Larry King would be fighting to give him air time. Born in Wales in 1841 to a farmer and an unmar-

81

ried woman, John lived with his maternal grandfather until the grandfather died. From age six to fifteen, John lived in an English workhouse until the misery forced him to run away. He lived hand to mouth until signing on as a cabinboy on a ship bound for New Orleans. There a cotton broker took a liking to the young Welsh lad, adopted him, and gave him his own name, Henry Morton Stanley. Sadly, Mr. Stanley died just before the Civil War broke out and had made no provisions for the boy's care. Henry joined the Confederate Army—as did many young men—and was captured at Shiloh. Ironically, this survivor switched sides and finished the war fighting in the Union Navy.

Stanley established quite a reputation after the war as a newspaper correspondent. He covered the cavalry campaigns in the American frontier and a British expedition in Abyssinia. However, he was soon to have the "story of his life" and one that would make his name a household word around the world; Stanley would be remembered for four words.

By 1869, it had been assumed that missionary/explorer/physician Dr. David Livingstone was lost—if not dead—somewhere in Central Africa, a vast territory largely unexplored. The editor of the *New York Herald* hired young Stanley to find the good doctor—that day's equivalent of a scoop. Three years passed, with widespread newspaper coverage of his exploits, before Stanley could say to an astonished missionary, "Doctor Livingstone, I presume." Thereafter, the two men became colleagues and coexplorers. After Livingstone's death in 1873, Stanley carried on the great doctor's work in Africa.

In 1874, Stanley began a three-year expedition to chart the great lakes of Central Africa. During the period 1879 to 1884, Stanley opened the Congo River Basin and established trading posts along the river. Between 1887 and

1890, he led a rescue mission to find Emin Pasha, governor of Equatoria. This single adult opened the vast mid-continent of Africa to European explorers—and sadly, exploitation—although Stanley was not responsible for that. This expedition alone required him to travel some 1,600 miles up the Congo River and through 500 miles of jungle. He lost two-thirds of his men to disease, starvation, wild animals, and skirmishes with Africans most resistant to European explorers.

Stanley wrote that he was forced to humbly confess, "Without God's help I was powerless. I vowed a vow in the forest that I would confess Him before men." What kept him going against such outrageous obstacles? Not just a quest for fame. Stanley explained, "Civilized society rejoices in the protection offered it by strong-armed law. Those whose faith in God is strong feel the same sense of security in the deepest wilds."[9] Later, he explained:

> On all my expeditions prayer made me stronger morally and mentally than my nonpraying companions. It gave me confidence. Without prayer I doubt that I could have endured the flourishing of spears when they were but half-a-dozen spaces from me. I know that when I have called I have been answered, strengthened and assisted.[10]

Stanley went to Africa as a journalist, something like the Ted Koppel of his day, but he wrote in his diary at David Livingstone's death: "May I be selected to succeed him in opening Africa to the shining light of Christianity. May God be with me as he was with Livingstone. May God direct me as he wills. I can only vow to be obedient and not to slacken."[11]

Although Stanley eventually married—at age forty-nine—his major accomplishments were as a single adult. Henry Morton Stanley was relevant.

Raoul Wallenberg, Never Married

Remember Jesus' question to the self-nominated-for-greatness boys? "Are you able to drink of this cup?" In the biblical language, a cup was not only a drinking vessel; cup also referred to a person's allotted portion or destiny. In Jesus' case as in James's case, the cup meant death (Acts 12:2).

Raoul Wallenberg had a future. As a member of one of Sweden's leading financial families and a graduate of the University of Michigan, he would have gone far in European banking circles. In 1944, the Nazis were working feverishly to enact their "final solution" on the Jewish race. Something had to be done. Into the arena stepped the thirty-two-year-old bachelor, at the request of the United States War Refugee Board and with the approval of the Swedish government. Already millions of Jews had died in Europe. What could one man do? "Just do something," Raoul was instructed.

Hitler's fanatic henchmen, sensing that the shift of the war would lead to their ultimate defeat, became determined to exterminate as many Jews as possible. Thus, in 1944, the Jews of Hungary were barricaded in Budapest. Time had seemingly run out for them.

Raoul Wallenberg worked night and day, to save as many Jews as possible. He pulled Jews off trains bound for the death camps, identifying them as Swedish citizens. He forged thousands of birth certificates and issued thousands of bogus Swedish passports. With his persuasive powers, he enlisted meager help from neutral embassies and from the puppet Hungarian government. He purchased buildings and declared them Swedish embassies and claimed Swedish sovereignty so that German troops could not trespass. Raoul even dressed Jews in German uniforms to confuse the Nazis.

In one bold move, Wallenberg bluffed his way into Nazi headquarters to confront a general: "If you allow this slaughter to take place . . . I will hold *you* accountable!"

"And *who* are you?" bellowed the general, "to tell me what to do!"

"I am only one man," Wallenberg glared, "but the world will remember. I have already notified my government that I am here."[12] So one angry general, no doubt to literally save his own neck from an eventual war tribunal noose, ordered German troops to stop the SS. As a result, some 100,000 lives were spared, including one sixteen-year-old who eventually immigrated to the United States.

But what happened to Wallenberg? Such heroics must have been rewarded. That's where the mystery begins. This much is known for sure: at war's end Russian troops in Berlin arrested Raoul. The Russians have offered two "official" explanations: that he was killed by retreating German soldiers; the other that he had died in 1947. However, across the years, a parade of survivors of the Russian gulags have testified that they saw and talked with the Swede.

In 1989, a crack appeared in the Russian explanations and *Perestroika* widened the gap. The Russians, however, could not believe that Americans would not "forget" this Swede after four decades. Barry Garron explained, "The very idea that a young, wealthy man would leave neutral Sweden to protect Hungarian Jews from death seemed incomprehensible to Soviet officials who had almost as little regard for Jews as Hitler's SS."[13]

Kati Marton put it more poignantly, "Why would a Christian risk his life for Jews?" unless, as the Russians concluded, he was a spy.[14] Remember, we have a selective memory about Christian attitudes during the late thirties and early forties with regard to rescuing the Jews from Hitler. It was not "our" issue, just as we argue today that involvement in Bosnia is not in our economic interests. Few were as committed as Corrie ten Boom and Raoul Wallenberg.

What a paradox! Fifty years after this single adult's disappearance people are still asking, "Where's Raoul?" and the Russians are still afraid to answer.

In 1989, the *Los Angeles Times* commented on the issue:

> He [Wallenberg] has succeeded in doing what few people in history have had the privilege of doing. Almost single-handedly, with enormous courage and dedication, he was directly responsible for the saving of the lives of tens of thousands of fellow human beings. For that he deserves, and has largely won, universal respect and remembrance. Even in the Soviet Union, a foreign ministry official has told Wallenberg's family, "he has become a hero."[15]

One former prisoner testified that he heard Wallenberg say, "I think I may have been forgotten by Sweden, and the rest of the world. I wonder if any of the people I saved still remember."[16]

At least one does. Tom Lantos survived Budapest, and is today a member of the United States House of Representatives. His first act as a member of Congress was to introduce legislation making Wallenberg an honorary United States citizen, only the second in history. President Reagan signed the papers in October 1981. Marton summarized his contribution: Wallenberg "instilled in thousands of Jews some kind of confidence in the future they had stopped believing in."[17]

Annette Lantos, another survivor, remembered and still remembers: "Here is one man who took on the nightmare and prevailed. He left us an incredible legacy. He did not just save our lives. He restored our sense of humanity and he restored our faith."[18]

What made Wallenberg risk it all? He was "imbued with a conviction," one biographer noted, "that anything was within reach, any goal could be met if one just applied oneself, and all of one's God-given gifts, to its fulfillment."[19]

This bachelor has not been forgotten. Today, the U.S. government annually sponsors the Raoul Wallenberg Award for Humanitarian Achievement. The Raoul Wallenberg Committee of Chicago sponsors the Raoul Wallenberg Humanitarian Award as a way of honoring "the lost hero of the Holocaust." The Israelis have remembered him in "Yad Vashem," the monument to the Holocaust where he is considered with another single adult, Corrie ten Boom, as "a righteous Gentile." The Holocaust Museum in Washington, D.C. is at 100 Raoul Wallenberg Place.

Raoul Wallenberg, a single adult, was relevant.

Clara Hale, Widow/Single Parent

It was a vintage Ronald Reagan moment: February 6, 1985. In the middle of his State of the Union Address, with millions watching on television, the president paused to draw attention to a woman he called "a true American hero," Clara Hale. Since 1969, "Mother" Hale had cared for more than six hundred babies born to mothers addicted to crack cocaine as well as congenital addictions. Most Americans had never heard of this single adult, but now the Congress, the Cabinet, and the Supreme Court stood to applaud the fragile elderly woman sitting near Nancy Reagan in the House gallery.

To make ends meet, as a young wife and mother, Clara Hale cleaned theaters in New York City late at night. At age twenty-seven, she was widowed with a daughter, age six, and a son, age two. To pay bills, she doubled up: cleaning homes during the day, theaters at night. She felt badly leaving her children alone so much of the time and began caring for other people's children in her apartment. Not only did she care for the children of live-in maids, Monday through Friday, but she began caring for foster children, seven or eight at a time. Today, many of those children are doctors and lawyers who remember the tender loving care of Mother Hale.

In 1968, she decided to retire and "just kinda take life easy." Her resolve was challenged a year later when her daughter, a sociologist, encountered a woman with a month-old baby in a Harlem park. This woman desperately needed help. Lorraine Hale told the woman to go to 154 West 122nd Street and promised, "It's a place where you can get help." Lorraine explained, "My mother has always been committed to the belief that there is a little bit of God in every person. She feels it is her responsibility to respect and honor everyone. I knew she would not turn that baby away."[20]

Before Clara Hale knew it, every "pregnant addict in Harlem knew about the crazy lady who would give her baby a home." Sixty days later, Clara had twenty-two addicted crack babies in her tiny apartment. Her daughter and son financially supported her initially; eventually, the compassionate resolve "just to love the children" began to attract governmental assistance and philanthropic donors. At age eighty-four, Clara still kept six babies in her bedroom. When they cried in the agony of withdrawal, she walked the floor with them, talked and sang to them. She rocked the babies and waited, knowing from experience that eventually the babies would smile back at her.

Mother Hale's philosophy of life was simple: she believed that "everyone comes into the world to do something" and that she "found what [she] was meant to do." She explained, "I love children and I love caring for them. That is what the Lord meant me to do."[21] Her eventual desire was to open Hale Houses across the United States. What would happen when she died?

> When I'm gone, somebody else will take it up and do it. That is how we've lived all these years. I am hoping that one day there will be no Hale House, that we won't need anybody to look after these children, that the drugs will be gone.[22]

Despite the media attention, Mother Hale explained, "I'm not an American hero. I'm a person that loves children."[23]

Clara "Mother" Hale, a single adult, was relevant.

Mary Ann Bickerdyke, Widow

What can *one* person do? We ask that question today, but at the outbreak of the Civil War in 1861, a forty-four-year-old single parent pondered it as well. Soldiers were not only dying from gunshot wounds, but also from the lack of nursing care and food. Mary Ann began collecting food supplies. Often she would show up in a church and pass a note to the pastor just before the sermon, asking for a donation. She began her "cow and hen" ministry, delivering as many as one hundred cows and one thousand hens at a time to field hospitals. One Union officer remembered Mary Ann Bickerdyke "as strong as a man; muscles of iron; nerves of steel; sensitive but self-reliant; kind and tender; seeking all for others, nothing for herself."[24]

She gained the nickname "Mother" because of her tenacity in fighting for the rights and needs of enlisted men, whom she called "my boys." Bickerdyke was not one to necessarily follow military protocol or governmental red tape if it inconvenienced her.

This was demonstrated at Lookout Mountain, near Chattanooga, Tennessee, on New Year's Eve 1863. Thousands of wounded Union soldiers waited for provisions and care in bitter cold. Fuel had run out; nothing could be done until morning. "Morning!" Mary Ann fumed. "These boys will be frozen to death by then. We need to do something, now!"

In her desperation, she stared at the log breastworks that had been built for fortifications. What use was this wood now that the campaign for Chattanooga had been won? Mary Ann ordered that the breastworks be torn down and burned to keep her wounded soldiers warm.

At daybreak, when the commanding officer discovered what had been done, he screamed at Bickerdyke, "Madam, consider yourself under arrest!"

Mary Ann looked up. "All right, Major. I'm arrested." Then in a most determined voice she countered, "Only don't meddle with me 'til the weather moderates; for my men will freeze to death if you do!"

Several hundred men survived that bitterly cold night because of one single adult's boldness. Among her other accomplishments was the establishment of military laundries. Previously, at tremendous cost, the bedding and clothing of wounded and deceased soldiers had been burned. Her laundries saved enormous amounts of tax money. As a volunteer, she fought vigorously for the recognition of women nurses in the Army. Despite protests by Army surgeons, General Grant accepted her idea. In one incident, when she secured the discharge of a drunk surgeon, he appealed to General Sherman for reinstatement. Sherman, Mother Bickerdyke's friend, responded that she outranked him and that there was nothing he could do. Bickerdyke marched with Sherman's troops to Atlanta and set up a large military hospital in nearby Marietta. Later, she was appointed to supervise the care of men who had been released from the horrible Confederate death camp, Andersonville.

Mother Bickerdyke was called "a cyclone in calico" because of her trademark gray dress and her seemingly boundless energy. She was known to leave the tent hospital late at night to wander the battlefields making sure no wounded soldier had been overlooked.

What energized this woman? One telling exchange at the Battle of Shiloh near Savannah, Tennessee, sheds some light. In her usual "take charge" manner she offended a male surgeon who thought women should either be prostitutes or at home tending children.

"Madam!" he arrogantly demanded of Mary Ann. "Under whose authority are you working?" Without pausing in her work, she answered, "I have received my authority from the Lord God Almighty! Have you anything higher than that?" The surgeon left her alone.

After the war, Mary Ann Bickerdyke encouraged the settlement of Kansas and hundreds of "her boys" complied. For awhile she ran a hotel in Salina. From 1870 to 1874, she was a missionary in the slums of New York City and taught Sunday school for the Salvation Army. The last of her life, Mary Ann spent in the West, acting as an attorney to help veterans and nurses secure their pensions. She was also involved in ministry to prostitutes in San Francisco.[25]

Mary Ann Bickerdyke, a single adult, was relevant.

Pierre L'Enfant, Never Married

Although Pierre had studied painting in Paris, he came to this country, as did many Frenchmen, to join the Americans trying to defeat the British. He attracted the attention of General George Washington when he designed an eagle emblem for Washington's Society of Cincinnati. In 1788, the American government commissioned L'Enfant to convert New York's City Hall into a federal capitol.

When the decision was made to create the District of Columbia, Pierre was hired to lay out the city. His design was imaginative: thirteen streets (named after the states) with two dominant buildings, the Capitol at one end and the White House at the other. He also sketched statues, columns, and obelisks, not just to commemorate the heroism of the patriots, but also to commemorate "those whose usefulness hath rendered them worthy of general imitation, to invite the youth of succeeding generations to tread in the paths of those sages or heroes whom their country had thought proper to celebrate."[26]

Although brilliant, L'Enfant was impatient and often lacked tact; more than one client declared, "You're fired!" The federal government dismissed him in 1792, and this single adult with an ego refused payment for his work up to that point. He died in obscurity in 1825, in the words of the hymn, "waiting the coming day."

On May 22, 1911, the most powerful men in Washington gathered around a grassy plot in Arlington National Cemetery for the reinterment of L'Enfant's body. In the eight decades since his death, a new appreciation had developed for the ingenuity of his design for the Capitol. That day Secretary of State Elihu Root observed:

> Few men can afford to wait a hundred years to be remembered. It is not a change in L'Enfant that brings us here. It is we who have changed, who have just become able to appreciate his work. And our tribute to him should be to continue his work.[27]

Remember the question that haunts many single adults, "If I die before I achieve?" Some achievements are recognized only after death.

Some single adults are not granted the privilege of enjoying wide public recognition and notoriety for their accomplishments during their lifetimes.

Pierre L'Enfant, a single adult, was relevant.

Thomas Dooley, Single Adult

Sometimes relevance happens coincidentally. Single adults do not get up one morning and say, "I think I'll become relevant today." Thomas Anthony Dooley III dropped out of Notre Dame in 1944 to join the Navy. After the war, he returned to complete his undergraduate degree and eventually the M.D. from St. Louis University. Then Tom rejoined the Navy. Events in French Indochina that would have far-reaching implications for the United States were just developing. The French colony was divided in 1954 into North Vietnam and South Vietnam. Lt. Dooley served as a volunteer medical officer in the South. In Haiphong, he supervised refugee camps housing 600,000 people after their escape from the Viet Cong. A *Washington Post* editorial proclaimed that Dooley's work was "the ultimate example of effective person-to-person contact with foreign people," of one man making a difference. Dooley's exploits were published in his best seller, *Deliver Us from Evil.*

In 1956, Dooley resigned his Navy commission, and with three corpsmen who had been with him in Haiphong, returned to that troubled area to establish a hospital in nearby Laos. Two years later he turned over the hospital at Nam Tha to the Laotian government and started a new one twenty miles away. In 1958, Dooley founded MEDICO to provide medical care for more remote areas. President Dwight Eisenhower wrote the young doctor, "It must be a source of heartened gratification to realize that

93

in so few years you have accomplished so much for the good of distant peoples and have inspired so many others to work for all humanity."[28]

By age thirty-three, this single adult, according to the Gallup organization, was one of the ten most admired Americans. His courageous example would prompt many young Americans to enlist in the fledgling Peace Corps. Dooley found time to treat thousands of patients and write two more best sellers, *The Edge of Tomorrow* and *The Night They Burned the Mountain*, again based on his work in Southeast Asia.

In 1959, this gifted humanitarian was diagnosed with cancer and returned to the States for surgery. After recovery, he immediately returned to Laos to plunge into a hectic schedule. In December 1960, when the cancer returned, Dooley fought back. He was fitted with a steel-and-leather harness, stretching from his shoulders to his hips, which he jokingly called "my iron maiden."

Tom Dooley found the Communists easier to fight than cancer. At age thirty-four, as he lay dying, with so many dreams yet to be fulfilled, Francis Cardinal Spellman visited him in his hospital room. Spellman later recalled, "I tried to assure him that in his thirty-four years he had done what very few have done in the allotted scriptural span of threescore and ten."[29]

At his death, in January 1961, few realized that his faraway world would soon be a quagmire for the American military. Dooley went there with a stethoscope and penicillin. The next generation of Americans went with the weapons of war.

Thomas Dooley III, a single adult, was relevant.

Paula Coughlin, Single Adult

September 6, 1992. Remember where you were that night? Paula Coughlin will never forget the convention she attended in Las Vegas. Paula, the thirty-year-old daughter of a retired naval officer, literally a "Navy brat," had grown up on a string of Navy bases. Few were surprised when she became a naval aviator.

"I've been in the Navy almost eight years and I've worked my butt off to be 'one of the guys,' to be the best naval officer I can and prove that women can do whatever the job calls for." She had to fight for advancement in a Navy overpopulated with neolithic minds; of admirals who longed for "the good old days"; with admirals who dared say that many women Navy pilots "are go-go dancers, topless dancers or hookers." Paula Coughlin ignored the double entendres, the invitations, the solicitations, and the harassment, and concentrated on perfecting her flying skills.

Tailhook quickly turned into a hellish nightmare when Lieutenant Coughlin and some two dozen other women were forced down a hallway gauntlet of grinning, mauling, fondling, assaulting, drunken male Navy pilots during the annual aviation convention in Las Vegas. The Navy's P.R. motto "an officer and a gentleman" was deeply tarnished; Rome in its debauchery had nothing on the U.S. Navy that night.

What did the Navy say, after the initial investigation? "Boys will be boys." What can women expect if they "invade" men's arenas of power and privilege? Besides, the military has long assumed there are only two types of women in uniform: "those who would provide for a man's needs and those who would not."[30] No harm intended, no harm done, the initial report concluded. The Navy's top brass concurred, anxious to find ways to protect their budgets from cuts in defense spending.

The brass, the Secretary of the Navy, and assorted admirals, however, didn't count on the tenacity of one single adult. Two days before another brave single adult, Anita Hill, had faced the "good old boys" of the United States Senate. Her example offered Lieutenant Coughlin the spark of courage she needed. Paula Coughlin went public, in her words, "putting a name and a face to this debacle" in Vegas.[31]

Tailhook is a blotch on military history. A tragedy. But not nearly as reprehensible as the attempts at cover-up by admirals with too much gold braid on their sleeves and too little steel in their spines. To pretend that it didn't happen encourages the next Tailhook. Great wrongs *can* be challenged.

An Ensemble of Difference Makers

In this chapter, we've looked at an ensemble of single adults who dramatically demonstrated that single adults can make a difference. They can be redemptive and relevant instruments of social change.

Unlike Muhammad Ali, none of these single adults proclaimed, "I am the greatest." To my knowledge none asked to be seated at Jesus' right hand. Just an interesting group of people: Mary Bartelme, Henry Morton Stanley, Raoul Wallenberg, Clara Hale, Mary Ann Bickerdyke, Pierre L'Enfant, Thomas Dooley, and Paula Coughlin. While some single adults sit around, like James and John, hungering for relevance and greatness, other single adults are in Godforsaken places, battlefields, ghettos, and lonely hells being relevant. The single adults I have highlighted in this chapter could have lived lives of comfort and ease. But they believed in God so completely that they dared say "Yes" to his summons to adventure. None of them was ever bored.

A single adult, Catherine Winkworth, translated Georg Neumark's awesome hymn, "If Thou But Trust in God," written three centuries ago. Consider the words:

> If thou but trust in God to guide thee
> And hope in him through all thy ways

He'll give thee strength whatever betide thee,
And bear thee through the evil days.
Who trusts in God's unchanging love
Builds on a rock that cannot move.

Sing, pray and keep his ways unswerving;
So do thine own part faithfully,
And trust his word, though undeserving
Thou yet shall find it true for thee;
God never yet forsook in need
the soul that trusted him indeed.[32]

The experience of these single adults calls to us on the eve of a new millennium to trust the God who, in Robert Seymour Bridges' words, "through change and chance guideth." Why? Ah, the poet explains, "God unknown, God alone, calls my heart to be his own."[33]

Two thousand years ago after a mother came to Jesus asking for special privileges for her boys, a lot of single adults are bound up in the pursuit of shallow greatness. Sadly, many are waiting on the sidelines for the "greatest" bandwagon to come along so that they can join up. Some things are never going to change if single adults do not do something about it. Opportunities still happen.

THE INVITATION TO RELEVANCE

Sometimes God asks single adults to be relevant. To step into the limelight and "to blow the whistle." To say "Enough!" To act as though what they do makes a difference.

The story is told of a great acrobatic stuntman who stretched a wire across Niagara Falls. Naturally, he attracted a crowd of excited spectators. They cheered as he paced the tightwire. On the American side of the falls, he called out to the crowd: "How many of you think I can push a wheelbarrow across to the other side?"

The roar was deafening: Yes! Bingo, a wheelbarrow appeared and he pushed it across the wire. Pandemonium broke out among the spectators.

He returned, "How many of you think I can push this wheelbarrow across . . . with someone in it?" The crowd roared: Yes! Yes! Tourists were congratulating themselves on having chosen this particular day to visit the falls.

"Now," the stuntman shouted, "who will volunteer to get in my wheelbarrow?"

Silence.

I heard a seminarian, Molly Smith, observe in relation to this story, that "faith is believing in God so completely and in his faithfulness we take our place in the wheelbarrow" and begin the adventure of faith.[34]

Will I find God's strength to be as precious, as sustaining as did Bickerdyke and L'Enfant and Mother Hale and Dooley and Stanley and Bartelme and Coughlin?

Jesus asked, "Are you able to drink from *this* cup?" While we all like the possibilities of greatness, true greatness comes in most unlikely arenas: rice fields in Laos, blood-soaked battlefields in Tennessee, small apartments in Harlem, hotel corridors in Vegas, or jungles in Africa.

If you want to be great, Jesus said and still says, you must be the servant of others. Laotians, crack babies, wounded soldiers, lost explorers, harassed races, assaulted women, lost explorers still need us. You may have to face down bureaucrats, Communists, Nazis, military brass, poll-watching politicians, whatever.

Hear the hymn's words: "If you but trust in God to give you . . ." Relevance. From the Latin. "To raise up."

I will act as though what I do makes a difference.

6

SINGLE AND REMEMBERED

George Anderson Wright has a good reason to be remembered. Wright was President of the United States. What! You don't remember President Wright? Well that may have been because he was only president for thirty minutes.

George Anderson Wright, mayor of Palestine, Texas, happened to be on board President Benjamin Harrison's train en route to Palestine. President Harrison was eating breakfast when an aide noted that people had lined the tracks wanting to see the president of the United States. Harrison looked up from his eggs and bacon and said to Mayor Wright, "You're about my height and size. Go out and wave to the people." When Wright protested he would fool no one, Harrison ordered, "George, you go wave."

So, while the president finished breakfast, Wright stood at the back deck of the train car and waved like a president. Of course, in 1891, few Texans had ever seen the president up close, only in newspaper sketches and pictures.

Once breakfast was over, Harrison took over the waving just in time, as the train pulled into Palestine; George Anderson Wright was demoted back to mayor. For years, Wright loved to tell folks about how he had been president of the United States for thirty minutes, because he sure wasn't going to be remembered as mayor of Palestine.[1]

We all ask, "Will I be remembered?" The question is especially common among single adults who realize that the right one may be permanently tardy.

In our culture a lot of negatives are attached to being remembered as an "old maid." Who wants to be remembered for the lack of a ring? I remember a professor in my doctoral work who, on the first day of class, without looking up from his roll book, began the roll call by asking, "Tell me one distinguishing characteristic I can remember you by."

When he came to my colleague, Frank Beard, Frank and the class laughed. Frank was the only African American in the class.

"Well, doctor, I think it's pretty obvious!" Frank retorted and finally the professor looked up and simply acknowledged, "Oh, yes."

How will you be remembered? How will I be remembered? Will our memory provoke an "Oh, yes"? You hope people will remember those things you want them to remember, rather than things you would just as soon forget.

The stark reality is that someone may live an honorable life for a half century, but should he slip up, particularly with a sexual impropriety, he will be forever tainted. There seems to be no statute of limitations on screw-ups. Wilbur Mills, representative from Arkansas, served in Congress from 1939 to 1977. Indeed, as chairman of the House Ways and Means Committee, he was one of the most powerful men in the Washington establishment. One biographer called him the "chief keeper of federal purse strings." Anything dealing with taxes had to go through his committee and that meant through Wilbur first.

Unfortunately, Wilbur got involved with a stripper named Fanne Fox. He frolicked with Miss Fox in the Washington Monument Basin one midnight while rather heavily intoxicated, and ended up front-page news. His long congressional career was ended by the public outcry. How was Wilbur Mills remembered? Well, not as a brilliant expert on the U.S. Tax Code.[2]

Sometimes, when we try to recall a name, we say, "Wasn't he the one who . . ." How will you as a reluctant single adult be remembered?

A SINGLE ADULT REMEMBERED FOR FAITH

Dag Hammarskjöld, the second secretary-general of the United Nations—a career Swedish diplomat and bachelor—attempted to transform the U.N. from a debating society on the East River to a force in world peace. He initiated the use of positioning neutral U.N. peacekeeping forces between warring factions, as he did in the Suez Canal crisis in 1956. What could have become an enormous global conflict, with Britain on one side and the U.S.S.R. on the other, was diffused.

Hammarskjöld, an innovator of "shuttle diplomacy," later perfected by Henry Kissinger, began the process when he flew to Peking to obtain the release of twelve U.S. airmen. A new generation of single adults is too young to remember this bachelor's death in a plane crash in 1961, while mediating a political crisis between the newly independent Congo and the secessionist Katanga province. Dag Hammarskjöld is just another hard-to-spell name in the history books.

Indeed, one biographer, Brian Urquhart, attributed some of the secretary's success to his singleness. "The absence of a benign tyranny of family life left him free to work and think at all hours, and to leave for anywhere at any time and at a moment's notice."[3] Hammarskjöld was a "born bachelor" and "it is impossible to imagine him in the amiable but time-consuming clutter of family life or in the genial distractions of a social circle."[4]

Dag was acutely aware of his loneliness; as early as 1958, he pondered life out of the public eye after retirement. In his journal he asked:

> Another few years, and then? Life has value only by virtue of its content—for others. Without value for others, my life is worse than death. Therefore—in this great loneliness—serve all. Therefore: how incredibly great what has been given me, what nothingness I am "sacrificing."[5]

Hammarskjöld assumed others wondered about the absence of sex in his life; then, as now, people were suspicious of the celibate. As Urquhart noted, many people (including some now reading this chapter) "find the concept of a man totally dedicated to his work, to intellectual and aesthetic interests and to spiritual experience, difficult to accept." The secretary-general penned a poem on the issue:

> Because it did not find a mate
> they called
> the unicorn perverted.[6]

Dag was hardly a social misfit. The secretary-general thoroughly enjoyed the company of his friends and was a wonderful host in his New York home. With the aid of a Swedish cook, Nellie Sandin, his hospitality was described as "superlative."

Dag Hammarskjöld provides a healthy role model for today's reluctantly single adult. Emery Kelen observed that the diplomat "suffered the agonies of his chastity; loneliness . . . was his hateful adversary." Kelen added, "He wrote of the envy of others in their partnerships. The very thought of sexual happiness turned his thoughts to the 'real bitterness of death': that one dies, while others go on living."[7] Hammarskjöld did not ignore his sexual desires but he did discipline them. Dag wrote his close friend, Bo Besknow, who had remarried in 1955, "Instead [of marriage] I have the light and easy warmth of contact with friends. . . . When I see other possibilities (like yours), *I can feel a short pain of having missed something,* but the final reaction is: what must be, is right."[8] Ah, the "short pain." Or, for many of us, the nursed pain. The pain we keep reminding ourselves not to forget. Dag Hammarskjöld wrote, "Pray that your loneliness may spur you into finding something to live for, great enough to die for."[9] What has your loneliness spurred you to do?

Theologian-biographer James William McClendon observed in his assessment of Hammarskjöld:

> We must note that it is the regular teaching of Christianity that *every* disciple take up his cross. The age-long problem is to find disciples who will take the summons seriously, but it is the irony of our times that when one man did so, he was accused of psychic derangement! In any case, Dag took the summons to walk the way of the cross to apply to him; that is, he believed he was called to a hearty and unselfish fulfillment of duty to his neighbors in the world community, even though that meant being misunderstood (as he was), even though it meant much suffering (as it did), even though he should suffer tragic death in that service (as, in the event, he has done).[10]

Paradoxically, three decades after his death, it is not for diplomacy that Dag Hammarskjöld is best remembered, but for his faith. In dealing with diplomats from all the world's religions and nonreligions, Hammarskjöld tried to steer a neutral course. However, he often slipped quietly into New York City churches for times of worship and reflection. After his death, aides found beside his bed a diary called *Vagmarken*, which revealed the depth of his faith. His diary was later published as *Markings* and is considered by many to be a devotional classic.

> I don't know who or what put the question. I don't know when it was put. I don't even remember answering. But at some moment I did answer Yes to Someone or Something—and from that hour I was certain that existence is meaningful and that, therefore, my life, in self-surrender, had a goal. And from that moment I have known what it means "not to look back," and "to take no thought for the morrow."[11]

Dag Hammarskjöld was most definitely the focus of whisper campaigns, periodically launched by his enemies because he lived in a time when most middle-aged, never-married males were assumed to be homosexual. Yet, he never fought back at his detractors. To a few friends, he explained that marriage and intense diplomatic service were, in his judgment, incompatible for him. Peacemaking came first.

Quiz time: Name the five other secretary-generals of the United Nations. Can't do it? Is it just coincidence that Hammarskjöld stands out?

He was a single adult remembered for faith.

A SINGLE ADULT REMEMBERED FOR INTEGRITY

The life of Jeannette Rankin illustrates the same concentration on values that endure. When she was elected to Congress in 1917, women could vote in only six states. In recent years, with so many women senatorial candidates, with women governors in Vermont, Oregon, Texas, Nebraska, Kansas, Kentucky, and the 1984 campaign of

Geraldine Ferraro for vice president, young single adults overlook the significance of those early political trailblazers. Jeannette, a former school teacher, had become an effective women's suffrage lobbyist while a graduate student at the University of Washington. She could have spent her life teaching school in rural Montana, but decided to do what no woman had done before: run for Congress. Besides, she quipped, what was the advantage of being able to vote if women could not vote for a woman? There was considerable debate over what to call her if she won. How could Miss Rankin be called congress*man*? Not to worry, scoffed her opponent, she didn't have a chance of winning!

Well, when the votes were counted, Miss Rankin *had* won. Jeannette took the nation's capital by storm, when she arrived to take her seat in Congress. President Woodrow Wilson hosted her at the White House; teas, receptions, press conferences were part of her whirlwind initiation to political and social life in the nation's capital.

But within four days of her arrival in Washington, she learned that part of a member of Congress's daily life is getting reelected.

War clouds billowed on the horizon. Her first major vote would be cast on the declaration of war against Germany. On April 6, 1917, the new representative sat through the intense debate on the declaration; the media, as well as seasoned politicians, speculated on how "the woman" would vote.

On the first roll call, after rancorous debate, she did not vote. The Speaker, "Uncle Joe" Cannon, admonished her—in the most patronizing of tones—"Little woman, you cannot afford not to vote. You represent the womanhood of the country in the American Congress. I shall not advise you how to vote, but you should vote one way or the other."

On the second roll call, when her name was called she stood and said, "I want to stand by my country, but I cannot vote for war." Because of the clamor on the House floor, the clerk of the House could not hear her. Male members, ready to be done with the business, shouted at her: "Vote! Vote!" The thirty-two-year-old single adult voted no and sat down.

Reporters dashed from the galleries to file stories that "the woman" had voted against war—ignoring the fact that forty-nine male members had also voted against the war declaration.

At 3:00 A.M. as she and her brother, Walker, who had managed her political campaign, walked to their lodgings, he could barely contain his anger.

"Don't you know," he growled, "you have just thrown away everything we have worked so hard to gain! Do you know, Jeannette, what they are going to be saying about you in the morning? You know you won't be reelected!"

Without hesitation she answered her brother.

"I'm not interested in that. All I'm interested in is what they'll say about me fifty years from now!"

The women's groups who had honored and toasted and hosted her only days before, publicly roasted her. She was an embarrassment, spokespersons declared, to the women's movement. Newspapers dismissed her as "silly and sentimental." Clergy demanded, in sermons on Sunday, that she resign. Another single adult, Carrie Chapman Catt, the national leader of the suffrage movement fumed, "Our Congress Lady is a sure enough Joker. Whatever she has done or will do is wrong to somebody, and every time she answers a roll call, she loses us a million voters."[12]

Much was made of the fact that she had been crying when she cast her vote. Someone asked New York Congressman Fiorello LaGuardia if that were true. Although he was seated near her, he answered, "I could not see, because of the tears in my own eyes."[13]

Walker was right; Montana voters soundly voted against her in the next election. So, the first elected female member of Congress was defeated. Over the next twenty years, Rankin turned down a marriage proposal from Congressman LaGuardia—because she didn't want to give up her independence—and became an active member of the ACLU. When branded a "Communist" by the Macon, Georgia, *Evening News,* Jeannette Rankin sued successfully and collected an out-of-court settlement of $1,000, as well as the editor's public admission that she was "a nice lady."

Political life does have its ironies. In 1940, as war engulfed Europe, Rankin was elected to the House and had the chance to stand in the House of Representatives and say, "I'm back!" Then she voted against the declaration of war against Germany and Japan in December 1941. Once again she was not reelected. Miss Rankin spent the rest of her life working for peace issues. At age eighty-seven she led an enthusiastic march down Pennsylvania Avenue to protest the Vietnam war.

Many argue that this young woman had had it all and had let it slip through her fingers. She could have had a comfortable, secure political career for the rest of her life, but Jeannette wanted to be remembered for her integrity, not her longevity in Congress. What Rankin realized was that it's easy to sacrifice the future on the altar of the immediate.

How is Jeannette Rankin remembered today? In 1985, sixty-eight years after her "no" vote, Speaker Thomas "Tip" O'Neill unveiled a larger-than-life bronze statue of her in the Capitol's Statuary Hall. She stands there as a reminder that integrity is rarely forgotten. I happened to be in Washington, D.C., during one of the House debates on the budget that forced George Bush to abandon his "read my lips" stance on new taxes. Behind the scenes there was great wrangling and posturing for political expediency. Daily, committee members working for a budget compromise had to pass Jeannette's statue. As I stood there, admiring the statue and the legacy, I thought, if only contemporary politicians had the same courage as had the single adult from Montana.

This single adult was remembered for integrity.

A Theologian on "Being Remembered"

Martin Israel, writing with a British viewpoint on singleness, addressed the issue of being remembered. He laments the efforts of a single adult, who, in pursuit of significance, strives obsessively to establish and protect his or her image in the world and to position oneself for future relevance.

> Everything he does has the final aim of exalting himself at the expense of others whom he uses quite unashamedly for his selfish purposes. . . . Ironically, the more he attains the more insecure he becomes, because he is entrapped in defending and maintaining that which is by its very nature ephemeral. By contrast, a person who is centered in the self projects his true identity wherever he finds himself for what he is—both a mere speck in the horizon of infinity and a living soul with God at its centre. In other words, he has no illusions about his insignificance as a personality but is constantly aware of the uniqueness of his contribution to the world as a servant of God. . . . He can radiate that unique presence to everyone and everything around him in an attitude of benediction.[14]

A SINGLE ADULT ON "BEING REMEMBERED"

Carmen Berry, a single adult, has written powerfully on codependency as it relates to the issue of significance. How many reluctantly single adults think: *If* I can be part of a partnership [a marriage] *Then*—and only then—am I somebody. Berry suggests that there are five billion people on planet earth, at the moment. How many are widely recognized of that five billion? A few have worldwide recognition: Clinton, Yeltsin, Princess Di, and Michael Jackson. Berry reminds us of the pained reality, "Most people alive in the world right now are not known to us and have no part in our lives."[15]

Let's go back a century. How many names would we recognize of people who lived in 1891? A president, a composer, a scientist, maybe a humanitarian. Suppose we asked for name recognition of people who lived 2,000 years ago, most people could come up with only two: Jesus Christ and Julius Caesar.

So what? If single adults try to gain significance by being remembered, whether as a celebrity or hero or saint, after death, Berry contends:

> We are in for big disappointment. Each of us will be remembered by a few people for some years after we die. Our lives will have made an impact on them. But sooner or later, those people will also die, and eventually we will be forgotten by all human beings. Once we are totally forgotten, what is the value of our lives? Where has the significance of our actions and words gone? Has it simply ceased to be?[16]

To further comprehend the issue, take a walk through an old cemetery and then through one of today's memorial gardens. In the former, you will find large, imposing tombstones and monuments, which give some indication

109

of at least the economic significance of the departed; in the latter, a polite equality exists: all have flat markers.

YOU WILL BE FORGOTTEN!

The painful reality is this: *you will be forgotten.* You can be page-one news today; page thirty-six tomorrow.

The psalmist wrote, "The steadfast love of the LORD is from everlasting to everlasting on those who fear him, and his righteousness to children's children" (Ps. 103:17). Ah, says the prooftexter, "children's children." Who will remember the childless single adult? Read on, "[And] to those who keep his covenant and remember to do his commandments" (v. 18). I interpret this passage to suggest that God deliberately includes single adults in this promise. No wonder Carmen Berry can suggest:

> While all human beings may forget us, God will never forget us. Just as God refuses to allow our sin to separate us from him, so God refuses to let us slip away into oblivion because of our mortality. It is God's love, not our deeds or words or fame [or marriage or children or assets or benevolences] that lasts forever. We are forever held in the tender arms of God's love.[17]

Now that is a promise you can take to the bank. The significance of a Christian single adult's life "Can never pass away, because God makes our lives a part of the everlasting, loving life of God. God accepts us and this acceptance is redemption."[18]

The Heidelberg Catechism, dating back to 1563, has brought comfort to many Christians. Its first question asks, "What is your *only* comfort, in life and in death?" The answer: "That I belong—body and soul, in life and death—

not to myself but to my faithful Savior, Jesus Christ."[19] I will be remembered because I *belong*.

A SOCIAL CRITIC ON "BEING REMEMBERED"

I was struck by the obituary of famed British author and social critic Malcolm Muggeridge, who himself said that he "never greatly cared for the world or felt particularly at home in it." What do you say about a man who achieved worldwide literary success? Malcolm himself responded to that question:

> I may, I suppose, regard myself or pass for being a relatively successful man. People occasionally stare at me in the streets—that's fame. I can fairly easily earn enough to qualify for admission to the higher slopes of the Internal Revenue—that's success. Furnished with money and a little fame even the elderly, if they care to, may partake of trendy diversions—that's pleasure. It might happen once in a while that something I said or wrote was sufficiently heeded for me to persuade myself that it made a serious impact on our time—that's fulfillment.[20]

What more could be said? Malcolm had fame, success, pleasure, and fulfillment. However, he also possessed a solid faith. He explained:

> Yet I say to you—and I beg you to believe me—multiply these tiny triumphs by a million, add them all together, and they are nothing—less than nothing, a positive impediment—measured against one draught of that living water Christ offers to the spiritually thirsty, irrespective of who or what they are.[21]

111

What an incredible statement of significance by one who definitely had significance! An old European hymn written by a single adult, Gerhard Tersteegen, captured the sentiment precisely:

> Though all the world my choice deride,
> Yet Jesus shall my portion be
> For I am pleased with none beside;
> The fairest of the fair is He.
>
> Be daily dearer to my heart,
> And ever let me feel Thee near;
> Then willingly with all I'd part,
> Nor count it worthy of a tear.
>
> O keep my heart and love with Thee
> Until my mortal work is done;
> And then in heaven Thy face I'll see,
> To be with Thee for ever one![22]

THOMAS MORE ON "BEING REMEMBERED"

In Robert Bolt's play about the life and trials of Sir Thomas More, *A Man for All Seasons,* More chides Richard Rich, the young teacher impatient for significance, position, wealth, and importance. More suggests that Richard go back to Cambridge. No, Rich says, "I want something for my work."

"Work?" More sputters.

"Waiting's work when you wait as I wait, hard!" Rich knew no one knew who he was or even cared. He was just another body at the Cardinal's court until the day the Duke of Norchester said hello to him. The initial surprise and pleasure at the recognition turned to cynicism and Rich dismissed the gesture with, "Doubtless he mistook me for someone."

When More points out that Rich had the offer of a post, a house, a servant, and fifty pounds a year, Rich responds disappointedly, "What? What post?"

"At the new school as a teacher," More reminds him. Rich retorts, "A teacher!" Of what importance is a teacher in the scheme of political power and court intrigue?

More points out that Rich could be a fine teacher—"perhaps even a great one."

"And if I was," Rich retorts, "who would know it?" In other words, what value is quiet unnoticed, unrecognized, unrewarded-at-the-moment significance?

But Sir Thomas has an answer.

"You, your pupils, your friends, God. Not a bad public."[23] Rich's words echo today in a culture held captive by celebrities. We too want notoriety and recognition for our work.

A WRITER ON "BEING REMEMBERED"

For some of us who are writers, one of the earliest institutions to impact our lives was the public library—a wondrous place with all those books! Years ago, near Chattanooga, there was a public library presided over by Mrs. Miller. We would probably never have known about her if it had not been for her impact on an eight-year-old named Elizabeth who loved books. Some librarians are there to check books in and out and to remind patrons to whisper. Other librarians, like Mrs. Miller, exist to encourage reading.

On one hot summer day, Elizabeth walked to the library to turn in her books and to check out some new ones. Books never lasted long with Elizabeth. When Mrs. Miller asked how many she wanted to check out, Elizabeth announced boldly, "Ten."

"Ten!" Mrs. Miller responded, with just the right amount of appreciation. "It's a good thing we keep getting new books. At this rate, you're going to have read all the books in the library!" Years later, Elizabeth recalled what happened next:

> Then came the blessed moment. Mrs. Miller reached into that wonderful, magic second drawer on the left that almost always held some books she had been saving. "How about this Caddie Woodlawn?" she asked me. "Or these two biographies, one about Jane Addams and the other about George Washington Carver?"
>
> "You know, Elizabeth," Mrs. Miller said as she handed me the latest treasures, "anybody who loves books the way you do is bound to become a writer. Why, you know what? I bet someday we'll have books you've written in this very library!"[24]

Elizabeth Harper Neeld asked, "Had I been moving toward becoming a writer ever since that day, and just hadn't known it?"

I don't know Mrs. Miller's first name or if she lived to see her prediction come true. I do know that Elizabeth Neeld is a gifted writer whose insights into widowhood have helped many, and somehow I think Mrs. Miller had some influence on the direction of her life.

Pick any profession—teaching, banking, medicine, acting—eventually you will be forgotten. People will say of you, as they have of history's long succession, "Whatever happened to so-and-so?"

People today are impatient. We want significance and we want it now, thank you. The point was underscored when Joseph E. Murray, 71, of Boston's Brigham Hospital, was awarded the 1990 Nobel Prize. His colleague E. Donall Thomas remarked, "It's an honor and a thrill for forty years of work. It's been a long, hard process." Murray added, "It's extremely gratifying" for all those years of developing transplant surgery, since that first experimental transplant at Christmas, 1954. "It means the work was worthwhile, I guess."[25] I wonder what he meant by "I guess"? Some have reached significance in their lifetime and discovered it rather a hollow achievement and have walked off the stage of the moment. The discovery remains, but not the discoverer.

Maybe Charles Spurgeon was right when he wrote, "A good character is the best tombstone. Those who love you, and were helped by you, will remember you when forget-me-nots are withered." If you want to be remembered, "Carve your name on hearts, and not on marble."[26]

A SINGLE ADULT REMEMBERED FOR COURAGE

As children, we pretended to be cowboys or soldiers and used our imaginations and limited historical knowledge creatively. In those days, we pretty much took for granted the historical significance of our heroes or heroines. Any questioning of the exploits or personal lives of Davy Crockett or Daniel Boone would have led to a fistfight. It was only later in upper-division college history courses that we would learn that our heroes' feet were often made of clay.

Many afternoons, we roamed our backyards refighting the Battle of the Alamo. "Remember the Alamo!" we yelled, piercing the quiet of the neighborhood and evoking more than one mother's threat: "Shhh! If you wake up the baby, I'll give you something to remember!"

That phrase "Remember the Alamo!" has been a rallying cry for many patriots. Remember Bunker Hill! Remember Guadalcanal! Remember Da Nang! A succession of places where Americans have heroically fought and where many have died.

But there might not have been a "Remember the Alamo!" if not for the exploits of a reluctantly single adult, who knew how a broken heart felt.

A band of courageous Texans were camped near San Antonio on December 4, 1835. Ben Milam had been sent by another single adult, Stephen F. Austin, founder of the Texas colony, to scout out the Mexican troops and to determine the possibility of the Texans taking San Antonio.

Ben Milam had every right to be bitter with life. This prominent merchant in Texas had often represented Texas' interests in Europe. On one trip to Europe, he searched London's finest stores and shops for gifts to bring back to his fiancée. When he returned home, her sister broke the news that in his prolonged absence, his fiancée had married another man.

Although devastated, Ben summoned his wits and said, "I am going to give you these things I bought for her; I haven't time for women anyway. My country surely must need me." The rest of Ben's life was devoted to one passion: freedom for Texas.

That cold December night, when he arrived in camp, he found many men ready to desert, to head home without fighting for San Antonio. Some argued that any attack would be suicidal against the superior strength of the Mexicans; others wanted to wait to fight until reinforcements arrived.

A once-in-a-lifetime moment erupted for Ben Milam. With the toe of his boot he drew a line in the Texas soil. Confronting the men, he demanded, "Who will go with old Ben Milam to San Antonio?"

Three hundred and one men crossed the line. The next morning the Mexicans were stunned by the furious attack of the emotion-charged Texans.

Ben Milam did not live to see the victory he craved. On December 7, he died of a wound from a Mexican bullet.

Eventually, as a result of the intense fighting, the Mexican army surrendered, and the ambitious Texans took a giant step toward the Alamo confrontation and eventual independence.[27]

Ben Milam has not been forgotten by Texans who know their history. Texas history buffs know that one man made a difference. I would not attempt to say that had Ben been married with 2.3 children he would not have been as brave.

But a single adult has been remembered for courage.

HOW WILL YOU BE REMEMBERED?

The Christian faith places a great deal of emphasis on remembering. The earliest chorus I remember learning was "Do Lord, oh do Lord, oh do remember me." When Jesus was dying, one thief dared request, "Jesus, remember me when you come into your kingdom" (Luke 23:42). Jesus didn't say, "I'm too busy dying." Jesus replied through intense pain, "Truly I tell you, today you will be with me in Paradise" (v. 43).

In my childhood church, a large oak table stood in front of the pulpit. Carved into its front were these words: "In remembrance of me." Many days, during long sermons, I would hang over the end of the pew and stare at those words. What did they mean? Paul records the root of the carving—Jesus' last meal with his friends.

> On the night when he was betrayed [Jesus] took a loaf of bread, and when he had given thanks, he broke it and said, "This is my body that is for you. Do this in remembrance of me." In the same way he took the cup also, after supper, saying, "This cup is the new covenant in

my blood. Do this, as often as you drink it, in remembrance of me." (1 Cor. 11:23-25)

In remembrance of me. Jesus—a single adult—did not want to be forgotten.

Today, the sacrament of communion will be observed, wherever his people gather: in cathedrals and in small, cinderblock country churches; with great pomp and ritual and with informality. Today, Jesus will be remembered.

I think if Jesus wanted to be remembered, it is all right for reluctantly single adults to want to be remembered too.

But it is essential to ask, "For what do I want to be remembered?" Then so prioritize our lives, that that will be the first thing that comes to the mind of those who would remember us.

Epilogue
A King and a Pauper

I have found it impossible," the young sovereign told a stunned nation via radio, "to discharge my duties as King as I would wish to do without the help and support of the woman I love." With that, in December 1936, Edward VIII abdicated the British throne in order to marry a twice-divorced woman, Wallis Simpson. I often heard his story as a teen because my minister used Edward's "sacrifice" to illustrate what one would give up for love and what Christ gave up for us.

As a teen, I found it hard to comprehend what the Duke of Windsor (as he was named after his abdication) walked away from. King of the British Empire. Only recently, in the research for *Reluctantly Single,* have I studied the entire text of his abdication address. Edward succumbed, of all things, to envy. He had jewels, crowns, servants, castles, prestige, some power. What more could he have possibly wanted? Something his brother, the Duke of York, had. Something many readers of this book desperately want.

A family. Listen to these words, *"He* [the Duke of York] *has one matchless blessing, enjoyed by so many of you and not bestowed on me—a happy home with a wife and children."*[1]

With that, the Duke of Windsor swore allegiance to the new king, George VI, and quietly slipped into exile.

Edward VIII gave up his throne to get married! Some Anglophiles contend it was not a particularly happy match.

What will you give up? I know what you're looking for, but what will you settle for?

I have been equally affected by the story of a pauper in my native Kentucky. I will let the brief newspaper article from the *Louisville Courier-Journal* tell the story of a disastrous fire on Valentine's Day, 1993.

> Two Eastern Kentucky brothers are believed to have died in a fire at their farmhouse in Floyd County.
>
> Ronnie Freeman had vowed to look after his younger brother, who had Down's syndrome and a mental age of 3 or 4, when their mother died in the late 1980s, said a family friend.
>
> Ronnie Freeman quit his job to care for his brother, preparing his meals, dressing him and attending to his every need, she said.
>
> Meek said that Paul Freeman would otherwise have required nursing home care.
>
> "But Ronnie promised his mother, and he kept his promise," she said.[2]

I am awed by such stick-to-itiveness. If there is such a word, Ronnie Freeman defined it. No doubt he was reluctantly single. To put someone else ahead of our own agenda is so rare in today's world. To spend one's life inconvenienced by a deathbed promise is hard to understand. What would he not give up in order to get married?

Did you see *City Slickers,* the movie about three friends on a modern-day cattle drive? Billy Crystal plays a man deeply depressed by his thirty-ninth birthday. His wife tries to console him by pointing out what a "great" life they have. But Crystal retorts, "I have a feeling that this is as good as I'm going to feel, as good as I'm going to look, and as good as my life is going to get. But frankly, it's just not that good."

Edward VIII decided life as king was never going to get better. So he stepped down.

Did Ronnie Freeman ever have a feeling that his life was as good as it was ever going to get?

The Japanese have a wonderful word *kaizen,* which means striving for continuous improvement. I have not written on *why* you are reluctantly single. I hope this book has given you encouragement to *kaizen,* to continuously strive for growth and improvement. But *jiudoka* is equally important: "the ability to stop the assembly line to correct a quality problem."[3]

While singleness is not an assembly line we all need time-outs to seriously examine our lives, our attitudes, our decisions, and our reluctance "to correct a quality [of life] problem."

Anybody can become unsingle, like Edward VIII. But it takes a unique person, like Ronnie Freeman, to befriend the circumstance and to make the most of a season called "reluctantly single."

We started this book talking about three types of reluctantly single adults: the floaters, the fighters, and the navigators. My hope is that as a result of our time together you have either become a navigator or strengthened your resolve to navigate this "stream" called single.

Notes

1. Single and Reluctant

1. "How Many Gays Are There," *Newsweek*, February 15, 1993, 46; "Few Men Are Gay, Poll Says," *Kansas City Star*, 15 April 1993, A1, A10; "The Power and the Pride," *Newsweek*, 21 June 1993, 54.

2. Joseph Frazier Wall, "Louise Whitfield Carnegie," in *Notable American Women 1607-1950*, vol. 1. (Cambridge: Belknap Press, 1971), 286-88.

3. Albert Bushnell Hart and Herbert R. Ferleger, eds., *Theodore Roosevelt Encyclopedia* (New York: Roosevelt Memorial Association, 1941), 329.

4. Ibid.

5. Sam Jones papers, box number 312, Woodruff Center, Emory University, Atlanta, Georgia.

6. Paul Gray, "What Is Love," *Time*, 15 February 1993, 51.

7. Ibid.

8. Stuart Mieher, "Men At War," *The Wall Street Journal*, 21 June 1993, R8.

9. Herbert B. Grimsditch, "Lipton, Sir Thomas Johnstone," *Dictionary of National Biography, 1931-1940*, ed. L. G. Wickham Legg (Oxford: Oxford University Press, 1949), 538-40; Alec Waugh, *The Lipton Story: A Centennial Biography* (London: Cassel, 1952), 26, 39, emphasis added.

10. Armistead Maupin, *Maybe the Moon* (San Francisco: HarperCollins, 1992), 57.

11. Francis Bacon quoted in *Respectfully Quoted: A Dictionary of Quotations Requested from the Congressional Reference Service*, ed. Susy Platt (Washington, D.C.: Library of Congress, 1989), 221.

12. Truman Capote, *A Thanksgiving Visitor/A Christmas Memory* (New York: Random, 1956), 77-78.

13. Dianne Aprile, "Valentine's Day: A Singular History," *The Louisville Courier-Journal*, 14 February 1993, H-1.

14. Ibid.

2. Single and Floating, Fighting, and Navigating

1. Christopher Winans, *Malcolm Forbes: The Man Who Had Everything* (New York: St. Martin's Press, 1990), 2-3.

2. Dan P. McAdams, *The Stories We Live By: Personal Myths and the Making of the Self* (New York: William Morrow, 1993), 12.

3. Billy Graham, untitled essay in *The Courage of Conviction*, ed. Phillip L. Berman (New York: Ballentine, 1986), 107.

4. Fenton Johnson, *Scissors, Paper, Rock* (New York: Pocket, 1993), 217-18.

5. Berman, *Courage of Conviction*, xi.

6. "Westminster Catechisms," *Oxford Dictionary of the Christian Church* (London: Oxford University Press, 1957), 1451.

7. Evelyn Underhill, in *A Guide to Prayer for Ministers and Other Servants*, ed. Rueben P. Job and Norman Shawchuck (Nashville: Upper Room, 1983), 320.

8. Susan Howatch, *Scandalous Risks* (New York: Knopf, 1990), 124-25.

9. Kevin W. McCarthy, *The On-Purpose Person: Making Your Life Make Sense* (Colorado Springs: Pinon, 1992), 96.

10. Ibid.

11. Johnson, *Scissors, Paper, Rock*, 221.

12. Hendrika Vande Kemp and G. Peter Schreck, "The Church's Ministry to Singles: A Family Model," *Journal of Religion and Health*, 20 (Summer 1981), 141.

13. Ibid.

14. Gregory Dix, *The Shape of the Liturgy*, 744 quoted in John Baille, *A Diary of Readings* (Oxford: Oxford University Press, 1981), 64.

15. "Maxey Dupree," *Kansas City Star*, 3 January 1990, C-6.

16. Emily Dickinson, "Not in Vain," *One Hundred and One Famous Poems*, compiled by Roy J. Cook (Chicago: Contemporary Books, 1958), 30.

3. Single and Shattered

1. Dietrich Bonhoeffer, *Life Together*, John W. Doberstein trans. (new York: Harper & Row, 1954), 97.

2. Alan Wolfelt, *Death and Grief: A Guide for Clergy* (Muncie, Ind.: Accelerated Development, 1988), pp. 74-80.

3. Linda Quanstrom, "And Then There Was One," sermon, First Church of The Nazarene, Kansas City, Missouri, 3 February 1992.

4. Concepts from Patrick Carnes, *Out of the Shadows: Understanding Sexual Addiction*, 2nd ed. (Minneapolis: ComCare, 1992) pp. 110-12.

5. Bill Huebsch, *A Spirituality of Wholeness: The New Look at Grace* (Mystic, Conn.: Twenty-third Publications, 1992), 98, emphasis added.

4. SINGLE AND BELONGING

1. Jonathan Yardley, "A Cause Worth Dying For," review of *Outside Agitator: Jon Daniels and the Civil Rights Movement in Alabama* by Charles W. Eagles, *Bookworld*, 6 June 1993, 3.

2. Mary McCay, "Darling, Ethel Percy," in *Notable American Women: The Modern Period*, Barbara Sicherman and Carol Hurd Green, eds. (Cambridge: Belknap Press of Harvard University Press, 1980), 25–26; "Darling, Flora," *The Continuum Dictionary of Women's Biography*, comp. Jennifer S. Uglow (New York: Continuum, 1989), 147-48.

3. Alexis de Tocqueville, cited in *Respectfully Quoted: A Dictionary of Quotations Requested from the Congressional Research Service*, ed. Suzy Platt (Washington, D.C.: Library of Congress, 1989), 21-22.

4. Carson McCullers, *The Member of the Wedding* (New York: Houghton-Mifflin, 1946), 1.

5. Helen Marshall, "Dorothea Dix," *Notable American Women: A Biographical Dictionary*, vol. 1 (Cambridge: Belknap Press of Harvard University, 1971), 486-89.

6. Mark Halasa, *Mary McLeod Bethune: Educator, Black Americans of Achievement* (New York: Chelsea House, 1989), 32, 34.

7. Gerda Lerner, *The Grimke Sisters from South Carolina: Pioneers for Women's Rights and Abolition* (New York: Schocken Books, 1971), 68-84.

8. "Carole Moseley-Braun. New? Yes. Novice. No!" *N.E.A. Today*, 11 (March 1993), 9.; "Carol Moseley-Braun," *People*, 28 December 1992, 86; "Outraged Senator Turns Tide Against Symbol of Slavery," *The Portland Oregonian*, 23 July 1993, A12.

9. "Ginsburg Hearing Dramatizes Shift on Judiciary Panel," *The Portland Oregonian*, 23 July 1993, A14.

10. Elizabeth Harper Neeld, *Seven Choices: Taking the Steps to New Life After Losing Someone You Love* (New York: Delta, 1990), 41.

11. Ibid., 58.

12. Janet Fishburn, *Confronting the Idolatry of Family: A New Vision for the Household of God* (Nashville: Abingdon Press, 1991), 63.

13. Ibid.

14. Timothy M. Phelps and Helen Winternitz, *Capitol Games: Clarence Thomas, Anita Hill, and the Story of a Supreme Court Nomination* (New York: Hyperion, 1992), 219.

15. Bill Groneman, *Alamo Defenders. A Genealogy: The People and Their Words* (Austin, Tex.: Eakin Press, 1990), 39.

16. Jeff Long, *Duel of Eagles: The Mexican and U.S. Fight for the Alamo* (New York: Quill/William Morrow, 1990), 340-41; *Women of Texas* (Waco: Texina Press, 1972), 65-66.

5. SINGLE AND RELEVANT

1. George Smith, *Henry Martyn: Saint and Scholar* (London: Religious Tract Society, 1892), 49.

2. Constance E. Padwick, *Henry Martyn* (Chicago: Moody Press, 1980), 99.

3. Ibid., 100.

4. Ibid., 108.

5. Source unknown.

6. June Sawyers, "Way We Were: 'Suitcase Mary' Leads A Crusade for Needy Girls," *Chicago Tribune*, 15 May 1988, C-10.

7. Ibid.

8. Ibid.; "Delinquent Girls' Court Opened by Miss Bartelme," *Chicago Tribune*, 5 March 1913, cited by Charles Winslow, *Biographical Sketches of Chicagoians* (Chicago, n.p., 1948), 153.

9. Thomas W. Wood, Jr., "H. Stanley," in *McGraw-Hill Encyclopedia of World Biography*, vol. 10 (New York: McGraw-Hill, 1973), 179-80; Walker Erdman, "Henry M. Stanley" in *Sources of Power in Famous Lives* (Nashville: Cokesbury, 1939), 140.

10. Ibid.

11. Ibid.

12. Barry Garron, "Hero of a Modern Exodus," *Kansas City Star*, 7 April 1985, 3F.

13. Ibid.

14. Kari Marton, *Wallenberg* (New York: Ballentine, 1982), 185.

15. "Editorial: He Deserves All Honor," *Los Angeles Times*, 20 October 1989, B-6.

16. Marton, *Wallenberg*, 205.

17. Ibid., 96.

18 Garron, "Hero of a Modern Exodus," 3F.

19. Marton, *Wallenberg*, 89.

20. "Clara Hale," *Current Biography Yearbook: 1985*, ed. Charles Moritz (New York: H. W. Wilson, 1985), 165.

21. Ibid., 167.

22. Brian Lanker, "I Dream A World; Clara McBride Hale," *Dallas Times Herald*, 2 March 1989, J-5.

23. Ibid.; see also "Spotlight: Clara Hale," *Modern Maturity*, October–November 1988, 18.

24. Harris Elwood Starr, "Mary Ann Bickerdyke," *Dictionary of American Biography*, vol. 1, pt. 2 (New York: Charles Scribner's, 1964), 237; see also Francis Willard and Mary Livermore, eds. *Women of the Century* (Detroit: Gale, 1967, reprint), 81-82.

25. Joellen Watson Hawkins, "Bickerdyke, Mary Ann (Ball)," *Dictionary of American Nursing Biography,"* ed. Martin Kaufman (Westport, Conn.: Greenwood Press, 1988), 32.

26. Alan Gowans, "L'Enfant," *McGraw-Hill Encyclopedia of World Biography,* vol. 6 (New York: McGraw-Hill, 1973), 420.

27. H. Paul Caemmerer. *The Life of Pierre Charles L'Enfant: Planner of the City Beautiful/The City of Washington* (Washington, D.C.: National Republic Publishing Company, 1950), 1. Caemmerer notes that although there was a tradition that L'Enfant was married, after careful census research in both Paris and New York City, no documentation has ever been found.

28. "Thomas A. Dooley, M.D." [Obituary] *New York Times,* 19 January 1961, n.p.; see also J. G. Feller, "Dooley, Thomas Anthony" in *New Catholic Encyclopedia,* vol. 4 (New York: McGraw-Hill, 1967), 1010-11.

29. Thomas A. Dooley, *The Edge of Tomorrow* (New York: New American Library Edition, 1961), v.

30. Scott Canon, "Shilts Looks at Gays in Service," book review for *Conduct Unbecoming* by Randy Shilts, *Kansas City Star,* 27 June 1993, J-9.

31. Ellen Goodman. "Navy Makes Right Moves on Tailhook," *Kansas City Star,* 28 September 1992, B-5; see also "Many Officers, Not Many Gentlemen," *U.S. News & World Report,* 3 May 1993, 44, 49.

32. Georg Neumark, "If Thou But Trust in God to Guide Thee," trans. Catherine Winkworth, *The Hymnal 1982, According to the Use of the Episcopal Church* (New York: The Church Hymnal Corporation, 1982), 635.

33. Robert Seymour Bridges, "All My Hope on God Is Founded," *The Hymnal 1982, According to the Use of the Episcopal Church* (New York: The Church Hymnal Corporation, 1982), 665.

34. Molly Smith, sermon, St. Andrew's Episcopal Church, Kansas City, Missouri, 27 September 1992.

6. Single and Remembered

1. Bob Bowman, *They Left No Monuments* (Dallas: Lufkiun, 1975), 45.

2. "Wilbur Mills," *Current Biographical Yearbook: 1992,* ed. Judith Graham (New York: H. W. Wilson, 1992), 639.

3. Brian Urquhart, *Hammarskjöld* (New York: Knopf, 1972), 26.

4. Ibid.

5. Ibid.

6. Ibid., 27.

7. Emery Kelen, *Hammarskjöld* (New York: Putnam's, 1966), 162.

8. Urquhart, *Hammarskjöld,* 26, emphasis added.

9. Dag Hammarskjöld, *Markings,* translated from the Swedish by Leif Sjoberg and W. H. Auden (New York: Knopf, 1965), 85.

10. James William McClendon, Jr., *Biography as Theology* (Nashville: Abingdon Press, 1974), 62.

NOTES

11. Hammarskjöld, *Markings*, 205.

12. Norma Smith, "The Woman Who Said No to War: A Day in the Life of Jeannette Rankin," *MS*, March 1986, 89.

13. Ibid.

14. Martin Israel, *Living Alone: The Inward Journey to Fellowship* (London: SPCK, 1982), 85, 87.

15. Carmen Berry and Mark Lloyd Taylor, *Loving Yourself As Your Neighbor* (San Francisco: HarperCollins, 1990), 86.

16. Ibid.

17. Ibid.

18. Ibid.

19. "Confessions," *Encyclopedia of Religion and Ethics*, vol. 3, ed. James Hastings (New York: Charles Scribner's, 1958), 866, emphasis added.

20. "Obituary: Writer Malcolm Muggeridge," *Christianity Today*, 17 December 1990, 46.

21. Ibid.

22. Gerhard Tersteegen, "Though All The World My Choice Deride," trans. Samuel Jackson, *Christian Hymns*. (Mid-Glamorgan: The Evangelical Movement of Wales, 1989), 622-23.

23. Robert Bolt, *A Man for All Seasons* (New York: Random House, 1962), 6-9.

24. Elizabeth Harper Neeld, *Seven Choices: Taking the Steps to New Life After Losing Someone You Love* (New York: Delta, 1992), 214-15.

25. "1990 Nobel Prize for Medicine," *Kansas City Star* 9 October 1990, 1.

26. Jon Johnson, *Courage: You Can Stand Strong in the Face of Fear* (Wheaton, Ill.: Victor Books, 1990), 91.

27. Don Ferguson, "Benjamin Rush Milam," *The Handbook of Texas*, ed. Walter Prescott Webb (Austin: Texas State Historical Association, 1952), 191.

EPILOGUE: A KING AND A PAUPER

1. Michael Block, *The Secret File of the Duke of Windsor* (New York: Harper & Row, 1988), 14-17.

2. "Brothers Believed To Be Victims Of Floyd County Fire," *Louisville Courier-Journal*, 15 February 1993, 4B.

3. Paul Duchene, "Three Little Words Lead To Success for Toyota," *Portland Oregonian*, 25 July 1993, E-3.